HOW TO MAKE BRAIDED RUGS

HOW TO MAKE BRAIDED RUGS

By

SALLY CLARKE CARTY

McGRAW-HILL BOOK COMPANY

New York • St. Louis • San Francisco • Düsseldorf
London • Mexico • Sydney • Toronto

TO JEAN AND BOB

Book design by Judith Michael.

23456789DODO798

Library of Congress Cataloging in Publication Data

Carty, Sally Clarke.
How to make braided rugs.
1. Rugs, Braided.   I. Title.
TT850.C26   746.7'3   76-49513
ISBN 0-07-010195-7
ISBN 0-07-010196-5 pbk.

Frontispiece:
Braided rug on quartz floor takes on elegance of its surroundings as it counterpoints antique game table, hand-carved mahogany chairs and contemporary sofa. Rug's muted colors pinpoint room's tranquility and create appropriate setting for alabaster chess board with olive- and rosewood figures. Oil paintings of New Orleans street scenes provide dramatic splash of color in otherwise quiet room.

CONTENTS

INTRODUCTION
AN EARLY AMERICAN CRAFT
FOR MODERN TIMES

I n the museums and private homes of quaint New England towns, one can still find examples of one of the most popular crafts of early American times—rug braiding. And for those people of today who would like to find a craft that is practical, inexpensive and simple to learn, rug braiding can be the answer.

A well-made braided rug, laced together properly so that no threads show, is reversible. For this reason it might well become a family heirloom, as it will wear twice as long as an ordinary rug. Warmth and softness underfoot are also characteristics of braided rugs. Remember, they were originally made to cover slate floors in homes with no central heating in a rugged New England climate.

For the economy-minded, the monetary outlay for equipment is minimal—a blunt-edged needle and several spools of carpet thread. There is no need for expensive yarns, frames or canvases.

Ecology enthusiasts will appreciate the recycling aspects of rug braiding. Old dresses, suits, coats, et cetera, that might otherwise

Rugs made expressly for the home in which they are used are a rarity in today's impersonal world. Here, antique furnishings and highly polished floor in the foyer of pre-Revolutionary house take on new beauty with addition of braided rugs. Braided mat, on candlestand at left, picks up colors of rugs.

end up in the scrap heap, can be used to fashion a truly beautiful rug for one's home. There is no need to buy new material.

It is possible, of course, to go all out and make a braided rug with intricate designs, beautiful shadings of complementary colors and spend large sums of money for new wool. The financial outlay would still be far less, however, than the cost of buying a handmade braided rug. There are mills and shops where wool can be purchased by the pound at impressive savings. Rug-braiding accessories are also available: braid-aids for turning and folding strips of material into a tubular strand, clamps for holding the braid taut on a table while working and reels to keep the strands from tangling. As you become more involved in your new craft, you may want to experiment with some of these various aids. Chapter 13 discusses them.

It is well to remember, however, that the nineteenth-century craftswoman had no gadgets to help her when making braided rugs. Thrifty homemaker that she was, she utilized the scraps left over from garments for members of the family. One can almost visualize such a family on a cold New England night, sitting before the fire with one child holding the strands as the mother braided, another tearing the material into proper widths and a third sorting out the various colors of wool for the new rug they would all enjoy.

Even the modern-day family could emulate such togetherness. Children especially, with their uninhibited flair for color and design, have more imagination than one would suspect when it comes to ideas for fashioning dad's old suits and mom's old coats into a truly outstanding rug. One can make it a more rewarding family project by singling out an inconspicuous section of the rug and unobtrusively but clearly stitching the names of all who worked on it and the date of its completion. Who wouldn't want to be part of such an unusual record for posterity?

Once you've started your braided rug, don't become discouraged by the friend or neighbor who tells you, "That's not the way my grandmother used to do it."

Because rug braiding is not an exact craft, one could talk to ten different individuals and hear ten different ideas on the proper method for making a braided rug. All are good. Most produce excellent results. This book offers a variety of suggestions not only for braiding and lacing but also for preparing material. Use those methods which seem easiest for you or experiment and decide which method produces results you like best.

And always keep in mind the New England woman of yesterday fashioning a bit of beauty and warmth for her home. She worked quietly, unhurriedly, with simple tools and scraps because nothing else was available. Today, the results of her work are museum treasures.

*Braided rug, made entirely from discarded wool clothing by
Jean Gardner, projects friendly Midwestern welcome in
entry of family's country home, Castle Park, Michigan.*

CHAPTER 1
HOW TO USE THIS BOOK

How many times have you become frustrated with the directions given for assembling a child's toy or for making a simple home repair? Perhaps you've even tried to make a braided rug after reading an article on the subject and wondered why yours didn't turn out like the one pictured in the magazine. The women's magazines in particular have often been guilty of promising too much with too little instruction. In some instances they have even given directions and accompanying illustrations that contradict each other. No wonder the poor reader is confused.

Rug braiding is easy, if you know what to do. And if you don't know what to do, the simple instructions in this book will soon have you excited about the craft. Diagrams and photographs further clarify many of the directions.

Each chapter offers techniques and ideas from rug braiders throughout the country. Some are teachers. Their shared knowledge proves one thing: No one person has the last word on rug braiding. There are many different ideas on the subject. Select those easiest for you and your specific needs. Most important of all, enjoy your craft and don't try to absorb too much at once.

In addition to clear, illustrated directions, this book tells you the *why* of what you're doing. Too often the beginner is told to do something in a certain way for no apparent reason or without adequate explanation. Once the craftsperson understands that the various steps in rug braiding are merely common sense, the process is no longer a mystery. It becomes clear and logical.

FOR THE BEGINNER

Be Aware of Your New Craft

Don't think for a moment that you're making an ordinary floor covering. Braided rugs have a history and a tradition that makes them very special. Chapter 2, *Creating an Heirloom*, will give you insights on the uniqueness of your craft. Read it over. It will provide you and your family with a new appreciation for your finished rug.

Start Out Simply

Every rug braider interviewed for this book made her first rug with recycled materials. Some still do. For all of them, that first rug was a learning experience, and if there were mistakes, they had the satisfaction of knowing they hadn't wasted money on new wool.

Chapter 3, *From Rags to Riches*, suggests many possibilities for obtaining used wool. If you're still not satisfied with the amount you have, consult Chapter 4, *Guidelines for Buying New Wool*. It offers advice from experts on what to look for when buying rug wool and how to plan buying trips for bulk wool with a minimum of time and effort. When you're ready to purchase material from some of the retail and mail-order firms listed at the end of this book, the knowledge will also enable you to produce beautiful rugs with the new wool at a relatively low cost.

Decide Where Your Rug Will Be Used

Size, shape and even color of your rug are all dictated by where you want to use it. If you know what size you want, check Chapter 5, *How Much Wool*, to get an idea of the amount of material you'll need. Have all the wool on hand before you start.

If you're not sure how your rug will look in a specific setting, study some of the photographs in Chapter 15, *Adapting the Braided Rug to Specific Decors and Needs*. There are pictures of braided rugs in every room of the house and in decors ranging from very traditional to very contemporary.

Prepare Your Material

This step, described in Chapter 6, *Selecting and Preparing Material*, is most important for the beauty and wearability of your rug. Do you know which materials are best for rug braiding, and which give disappointing results? Chapter 6 evaluates textures and fabrics best suited for your new craft. Read it over, follow the guidelines, and your rug braiding and lacing will go very fast.

This chapter also offers suggestions for "lap" work which can be done away from home while you're attending meetings or traveling on a train or bus.

Before tearing the material in strands for braiding, you may want to take a look at Chapter 7, *Narrow vs. Wide Braids*. It's a short chapter and gives the pros and cons of a friendly argument that's been going on among rug braiders for generations. Just remember: It's your rug and you can have any width braid you want.

The wider strands are easier to handle, however, and you may want to start out this way. Most rug braiders do and eventually graduate to the narrower braids as they become more proficient in the craft.

Begin Braiding and Lacing

There's a right and a wrong way to braid. Chapter 8, *Braiding*, has directions and photographs for the do's and don'ts of good braiding. While you don't have to be a perfectionist, it's just as easy to make a firm, even braid as a loose, irregular one. Your rug will show the difference and, if made with a firm braid, will last longer. This chapter also gives simple illustrated directions for eliminating the most common complaint of novice rug braiders, a bulge in the middle of the rug. Whether you're making a round, oval or square rug, complete and easy instructions and diagrams will help you fashion one you can be proud of.

Another complaint, and one that has discouraged many a beginner, is buckling or cupping of the rug. There's a very simple way to avoid this, merely by changing the pattern of your lacing. Chapter

9, *Putting the Rug Together*, describes it fully with accompanying illustrations for greater clarity. In addition, there are instructions for avoiding abrupt color changes in a rug. The chapter also includes directions for finishing off the rug with a neat, tapered ending.

AS YOU PROGRESS

Think About Color and Design

Once you see for yourself how easy the basics of braiding and lacing are, you'll be able to turn your attention to other aspects of the craft. The simplest and most traditional of the braided rug patterns, the "hit-or-miss," is probably the best one to start with. There are many ways to make this rug, and Chapter 10, *How to Combine Colors Effectively*, includes several.

Color is very important in braided rugs. You make designs with color, give character to your rugs with it. The beauty of furnishings and floors can be enhanced with proper color. So many people, however, are afraid of color and cling to uninspired and "safe" shades. This chapter describes not only what specific colors will do but how they react on each other. There are also directions for the monochromatic rug and hints for effective shading.

Once you discover what color can do for your rug, you'll become interested in design. As you go through Chapter 11, *Distinctive Designs*, you'll find there's no great mystery about pattern; it's achieved by color. Sometimes it's done by the placement of contrasting colors within the braid itself. Or rows of braids can relate to each other to produce specific designs. Chapter 11 contains row-by-row directions for several traditional designs that rug braiders have been using for generations.

Personalize Your Rug

Few crafts offer as many opportunities for personalizing the finished product as rug braiding does. When you've mastered the basics of braiding and lacing and achieved confidence in the use of color and design, you're ready to personalize each rug you create. Chapter 12, *How to Personalize a Rug*, has many suggestions to help you see individualities which can very easily be worked into a rug.

BROADENING YOUR HORIZONS

Braiding Accessories

In spite of the many pros and cons about rug-braiding accessories, most craftspeople agree—they do save time. For example, if you use the Vari-Folder Braid-aids described in Chapter 13, *Braiding Accessories*, you can eliminate many of the steps necessary for preparing material. These devices automatically turn in all the raw edges of your strips. In addition, you can use three different weights of wool in one braid with uniform results. And of course, if you can work faster and easier, you can make that many more braided rugs.

The chapter will be meaningful to you as you become more experienced in your craft. Most veteran rug braiders eventually invest in accessories including special lacing thread and clamps for holding the braid taut on a table while working.

Dyeing Fabrics

Many people are reluctant to use packaged dyes and perhaps with good reason. Images of boiling pots, steamy kitchens and stained hands come quickly to mind. However, dyeing is much easier than it was years ago. Methods have improved and there's a vast array of colors from which to choose. If you can't find a certain color, pick up a package of dye and read over Chapter 14, *Color Creativity with Dyes*. It's exciting to see what can be done with drab, uninteresting fabrics. Once you try it, you'll have a greater selection of colors to work with and may want to go back to Chapter 10, *How to Combine Colors Effectively*.

Try New Ideas

The photographs throughout this book should certainly convince you of one thing: The concept that the braided rug is only suitable for an Early American setting is a very narrow one. Chapter 15, *Adapting the Braided Rug to Specific Decors and Needs*, provides ample evidence that the braided rug is suitable for modern as well as traditional settings. Chapter 16, *Other Ideas with Braids*, shows its versatility in the bedroom and bathroom as well as other parts of the home. There are also interesting suggestions for gifts, chair seat covers and table mats.

Become Knowledgeable on the History of the Craft
Anything you do as a craft takes on a greater meaning when you have background information on the subject. You may be surprised about the history of the braided rug as revealed in Chapter 17, *Treasures of Yesteryear*. Did you know, for instance, that it does *not* date back to Colonial times and that very few homes had any kind of floor covering in the eighteenth century?

Viewing the braided rug from an historical perspective can be fascinating, especially when one considers how and why it keeps reappearing on the American scene.

Chapter 18, *Braided Rugs of Nantucket Island*, centers on one section of New England where the craft has always been very much alive. The photographs, particularly, offer visual evidence of why the braided rug continues to be a Nantucket favorite.

WHEN YOUR BRAIDED RUG IS FINISHED

Once you've completed your rug, you'll be concerned with the practical considerations of its cleaning, repair and possible storage. Chapter 19, *Easy Care of Braided Rugs*, draws on the experience of many individuals. Depending on your temperament and schedule, evaluate their suggestions for your own use.

PROSPECTS FOR THE FUTURE

Most of the rug braiders quoted in this book were self-taught. Many are now instructors. Others do custom work. Certainly this is a craft that is salable, and Chapter 20, *Turning a Hobby into Profit*, tells you how to go about marketing your skills and what to charge. It offers advice about the pitfalls of consignment and what to expect from students. But whether you'd like to teach or take orders for custom-made rugs, this chapter will launch you successfully.

A FINAL WORD

Take your new craft in stride, one step at a time. And don't become so concerned with perfection that you lose your enthusiasm. The basics are simple and easy to learn. Once you've grasped them, use your imagination in creating the rug of your choice.

CHAPTER 2
CREATING AN HEIRLOOM

Have you ever seen something in another person's house that was outstandingly beautiful or different and wished you might have something similar? Perhaps it was a precious piece of porcelain or an original oil painting hanging over the fireplace or maybe an elegantly fashioned silver tea service.

At one time, only the wealthy could enjoy the luxury of beautiful surroundings. But today, with a little imagination and a minimum amount of skill, homes can be made distinctive without great outlays of money. In the past few years particularly, more and more homemakers have discovered that one can create beauty by returning to the crafts of an earlier age.

Besides the monetary considerations, there are other reasons for this trend. Some individuals have become craft-minded because they are dissatisfied with the blandness and uniformity of machine-made products. Others are disillusioned with the short life-span of mass-produced items. (How many things can one buy today that will last a lifetime or be passed down to one's children and grandchildren?)

Light airiness of white wrought-iron furniture is further emphasized by sunlight and greenery. Narrow braids and stylized patterns in rug maintain feeling.

As needlecraft skills in particular are once more coming into their own, one finds touches of elegance in the simplest homes. Macramé shades, drapes stitched with crewel work or chair seats upholstered in needlepoint are only a few of the handcrafted items within reach.

Some people admire such beauty and wish they were as clever with their hands as a friend or neighbor. If you fall into this category or if you're seeking a new craft to complement some of the other hand-fashioned items in your home, rug braiding may be just what you're looking for.

RUG BRAIDING IS SIMPLE TO LEARN

Anyone who decides to make a braided rug needs no great talents or skills as a needleworker. There are no intricate stitches or patterns involved. By following simple directions, the unskilled beginner can easily put together a braided rug to be proud to use at home or give as a gift.

Basically, there are only three things you have to do:

1. Collect and prepare your material
2. Braid the material.
3. Join the braids together.

Interestingly enough, when your rug is completed it can be most dramatic looking and give no hint whatsoever of how easy it was to make. And if your work has a few slight irregularities, so much the better. They will enrich the rug with a quaint, hand-done appearance and add to rather than detract from its charm. The too-perfect rug loses its individuality and may even look like a department store purchase.

NO ARTISTIC TALENT IS NEEDED

What will make your rug distinctive is your own creativity. Few crafts offer such vast leeway for personal expression in design and use of color. Don't be discouraged, however, by lack of confidence in your ability. If you feel you have no artistic talent, this book gives simple and easy-to-follow guidelines for making the rug that best expresses your individuality and tastes. And in today's impersonal world, how many individuals can have rugs that are made expressly for the home in which they are used? Such custom work is not only rare but prohibitively expensive and will certainly be visible testimony to your talent as a homemaker.

BRAIDED RUG CAN LAST A LIFETIME

Beauty alone, however, is not the only consideration for making a braided rug. You'll also have the satisfaction of knowing you're creating something that will last. Some of the most beautiful braided rugs to be seen today are used as floor coverings for period restorations in the Shelburne Museum outside of Burlington, Vermont. Most of them were made about twenty years ago and are walked on annually by over one-hundred thousand visitors. Their mint condition testifies to their durability. Of course, rugs in the typical home of today would never get such wear in even several lifetimes, but it is encouraging to know that the time you spend making your rug will produce something of lasting value.

Braided rugs also have a way of aging gracefully. Like the patina on a piece of antique furniture, the older they are, the more beautiful they become.

ADAPTABILITY TO ANY DECORATING NEEDS

Perhaps what you're really interested in is something to add life to a humdrum room, or possibly a way to achieve unity and harmony in a badly laid out room. Here is where the versatility of the braided rug will surprise you.

Typically, it has been identified with an Early American setting.

However, by changing the shape or using certain colors, it can be adapted to any decor—traditional, contemporary or modern. And it can be used in any room. Chapter 15, *Adapting the Braided Rug to Specific Decors and Needs*, offers ideas and photographs showing a wide variety of settings in which the braided rug is an ideal floor covering. And in Chapter 16, *Other Ideas with Braids*, there are directions for making a cuddly kitten rug, perfect for the bedroom or bathroom.

A VERY PERSONAL CREATION

When making your rug, be sure to personalize it so that it will always be identified as *your* rug in years to come. (Chapter 12, *How to Personalize a Rug*, has several ideas on how to do this simply and quickly.) Members of the family often become very attached to the braided rugs that grace their homes. When children leave for marriage or an independent career-oriented life-style in their own apartment, don't be surprised if they ask for one of your rugs to help them set up housekeeping.

Clara Seaman, whose suburban Westchester, New York, home is filled with evidence of her needlework skills, tells the story of the braided rug she made for her daughter Virginia's bedroom many years ago.

"Virginia loved that rug," she recalls, "and when she left us to marry and begin her own household, she asked if she could have it."

The rug was to be the focal point in the newlywed's living room but was too small for the large apartment. And so Clara dug out some remnants of woolen material, began braiding and added several new rows of braids to enlarge the rug to the proper size.

RUGS CAN BECOME FAMILY HEIRLOOMS

It is this sense of the personal that often endears a rug to the person who made it and to members of the family. In any home, floor coverings are basic furnishings, but the lasting charm of a homemade rug, one that represents time, interest and individual artistry of some family member, is a special source of pride and satisfaction to the entire family. Your own ingenuity will create something that will not only give beauty and service for many years to come but that can become a family heirloom.

Elizabeth Whidden of Larchmont, New York, who left her beloved Maine years ago, still treasures the braided rug her grandmother made over half a century ago. She has only to look at it and the picture postcard scenes flash through her mind. Windswept coasts, snowy sleigh rides to the country for Thanksgiving dinner and cozy winter evenings in front of the fire are beautiful memories linked with her grandmother's rug.

MODERN MATERIALS AND SKILLS PRODUCE A BETTER RUG

While yesterday's rugs are often today's treasures, the modern homemaker can produce a much more beautiful and durable rug than her nineteenth-century counterpart. The crafter of today has a wider selection of colors and designs from which to choose when fashioning a rug. There are many varieties of plaids and tweeds to give interesting textures to a creation. Colorfast dyes will produce that difficult-to-find shade one may be looking for. And best of all, there is the benefit of the experience and know-how of generations of homemakers who have passed down their hints and shortcuts for making braided rugs.

The next chapter will start you on your way to this satisfying and interesting craft. As you follow the simple steps and begin your rug, you'll be doing more than making a unique floor covering to enhance and beautify your surroundings. You'll be creating an heirloom for generations to come.

CHAPTER 3
FROM RAGS TO RICHES

When his wife began searching for rug-braiding material, one man became so alarmed at her zest for raiding the family clothes closets that he seriously considered hiding his best suits.

Anyone who has made braided rugs can sympathize with the woman's enthusiasm. Wool is not as available as it was years ago and some of the best is to be found in men's clothing. And what better place to start looking for recycled materials than one's own home?

When people become more deeply involved in the craft, however, they soon discover they must look elsewhere for fabric. Rugs require a great deal of material. Tell everyone you know about your new craft and ask them to save all discarded wool clothing. Don't forget to mention blankets and bathrobes. Old army and navy uniforms are another excellent source of long-wearing material suitable for rugs.

Some of the heavier cottons can also give good service if used for a small rug. But don't mix cotton and wool. The rug will wear unevenly. Barbara Fisher, a rug-braiding teacher from Holbrook, Massachusetts, began the craft over thirty years ago and often cut up old slipcovers. If you do this, use the material in the back that isn't worn. Heavy drapery material is also good.

Wide braids give homier, more traditional look to rug.

No matter how worn a garment may appear to be, don't discount its use. Clothes wear unevenly. A jacket with threadbare elbows often has material in the front and back that would be perfect for a rug. Impress this point on your friends when you ask them to save wool clothing. Tell them you'll be the judge of whether or not something is usable.

Never discard anything because you don't care for the color. While the rug braider who works strictly with recycled materials is more limited, she or he can still obtain a wide selection of exciting colors by dyeing. Chapter 14, *Color Creativity with Dyes*, covers this subject thoroughly and describes how different dyes react to different colors in fabrics.

When you've alerted all your friends and relatives to what you want and have diligently canvassed the neighborhood, here are a few ideas for other sources of used wool.

THRIFT SHOPS

Junior League
This organization maintains thrift shops in many cities and suburban areas. Find out if there's one near you and ask to be placed on the mailing list. Several times a year there are closeout sales, and one can often pick up suits or overcoats for as little as fifty cents.

Hospitals
Many hospitals have thrift shops. Ask the manager if they ever have closeout sales on clothing. These shops usually don't have mailing lists, but you can call periodically to see what's available.

Salvation Army
Check the phone book for the one nearest you or call the main office and ask which shop has the largest selection of used clothing. Again, ask about closeout sales.

Goodwill Industries

Here is another excellent source for used clothing, particularly men's suits and overcoats. Ask the manager to set aside those items that seem unwearable. Remember, no matter how ragged they appear, parts of the back and inner sleeves are often usable for rug braiding.

Churches

Some churches maintain a year-round thrift shop which is open one or two days a week. Others have periodic rummage sales with excellent buys. Watch the newspapers for ads of these sales.

The secret of getting good buys at thrift shops is—haunt them. One can go several times and find nothing. But there's always a chance that you'll come away with a windfall. Get to know the managers. Tell them what you're doing. They may have other ideas for inexpensive sources of used clothing.

DECORATORS

If there's an interior decorating shop nearby, pay a visit and tell them about your rug braiding. These shops often have fabric ends that they'd be happy to give you. Not only will the material be new but it is usually of the finest quality. Specify that you're particularly interested in wools.

DRY CLEANERS

Sometimes dry-cleaning establishments have unclaimed merchandise that they're willing to sell. Generally, there are no set prices. Talk to the manager and strike a bargain.

MOVING AND STORAGE COMPANIES

These firms often sell wardrobes with clothes that are unclaimed.

You'll find many listings in the yellow pages of your phone book. Make it clear, however, that you'll buy nothing sight unseen.

GARAGE SALES

Who knows what one will find at a garage sale? Maybe a huge box of clothing, no longer wearable, will end up as a beautiful rug in your home. And chances are you'll get it for pennies.

TAILOR SHOPS

Tailors are usually delighted to think that their cuttings and scraps will be put to good use. However, they have very little wool. Synthetics don't wear well, but you might want to use them for a hit-or-miss chair seat cover. For more ideas on how to use tailors' cuttings, see Chapter 16, *Other Ideas with Braids*.

If you feel you've exhausted all sources, the next chapter offers guidelines on what to look for when buying rug wool in bulk. Read it before you purchase material from a retail source in your vicinity or from one of the many mail-order firms listed at the end of the book. Remember, however, it is possible to make a braided rug entirely from recycled materials. Jean Gardner, of Oak Park, Illinois, made ten braided rugs, all sizes and shapes, for the family's country home in Michigan.

"I never bought a thing," she said, "except for once when I picked up two wool scarves at a church bazaar for twenty-five cents."

Pewter kettles and plates, cast-iron skillet and pots, and wicker baskets stand out against white bricked fireplace. Color relief in Early American kitchen is provided by bowl of bright red apples on stool and hit-or-miss braided rug.

CHAPTER 4
GUIDELINES FOR BUYING NEW WOOL

Most people who sew have a favorite fabric shop. In many instances, the owner alerts them to upcoming sales and gives them preferential treatment when there are good buys. But the needs of rug braiders are very special. They require vast amounts of material and are making something that will get a great deal of wear.

Beginners are often tempted to use acrylics because the fabrics come in such a wide range of rich colors and textures. But if there is one consistent piece of advice offered by rug braiders throughout the country, it is this: Don't use acrylics. (The exception might be chair seat covers or casual rugs that won't be placed in heavily trafficked areas.) Remember, you're not making a dress or a coat to be worn for one or two seasons. A braided rug represents an investment of time and talent. Use the best, most durable materials available. They needn't cost any more if you're aware of some of the excellent buys on new wool.

Bulk wool is less expensive when you take what's available and don't specify color choice. However, this needn't limit you in making color coordinated rugs. Unlike most synthetics, wool takes dye beautifully. Chapter 14, *Color Creativity with Dyes*, gives complete

Dark border frames rug, ties it all together.

instructions for easy dyeing. And when you see the color charts from the various dye manufacturers, you'll realize your color range with wool is limitless.

Before you write or visit the firms listed at the end of the book, here are some facts to guide you when buying wool.

THREE TYPES OF WOOL

George Dorr, of the Dorr Woolen Mills in Guild, New Hampshire, is well known throughout the industry for the excellent wools his firm produces for rug hooking and braiding. He suggests that buyers be aware not only of wool content but the condition or type of wool.

New Wool or Virgin Wool
This label refers to 100 percent wool converted into yarn or fabric for the first time.

Reprocessed Wool
Samples, cutting-table scraps and mill ends that are collected and made into other fabrics become reprocessed wool. While such wool has never been worn or used, it does not have the wearing qualities of 100 percent wool. Each process the material goes through weakens the fabric.

Reused Wool
Considered the lowest quality of wool, reused wool is exactly what the label says. Old rags and clothes that have been worn are collected, cleaned and converted into fabric. They are usually blended with some new wool for necessary strength.

WHEN YOU BUY WOOL BY THE POUND

Color Selection is Sometimes Limited
There are really some incredible bargains when one purchases wool

by the pound. However, as previously mentioned, there is not always the color selection one would like. But generally there are a great many whites, beiges and grays which can be dyed later to produce exactly the shade you want. Also, a pale pink can become a blush rose or an earth rust. Pale blues are good for dyeing if you can't find the greens you need.

Think Ahead

Betty Campbell, a rug-braiding teacher from Allentown, Pennsylvania, offers this advice when buying wool by the pound.

"When I'm buying for the rug I'm working on, I'm already thinking about the next one," she says. "When I see colors that might be good for another rug, I buy them."

She accumulates a great deal of fabric this way but finds it easier than going back several times for specific colors.

CHECK THE POSSIBILITY OF SOURCES NEARBY

If you've never purchased bulk wool before, you may be unaware of sources right in your own area. Check the yellow pages of cities and towns nearby. Look under the following headings:

1. Mill Ends
2. Waste—Cotton, Wools, Synthetics, etc.
3. Woolen Goods—Wholesale
4. Woolen Mills

Even if these firms don't have what you want, they can often lead you to others that do.

Be fussy about the quality of wool you buy and, when dealing with the firms listed at the end of the book, check on the different types of wool they sell. Avoid reprocessed wools. They will soon show wear.

Discarded wool clothing, braided into rug by Jean Gardner of Oak Park, Illinois, captures family memories of years gone by.

CHAPTER 5
HOW MUCH WOOL

"One of the things I like about rug braiding," says Ann Killen of Nantucket Island, "is that you don't always have to be exact."

Probably nowhere is this lack of exactness more evident than when the would-be rug braider tries to determine the amount of material needed for a rug. There are no precise formulas or rules as in cooking or sewing. And with good reason.

No two individuals braid alike and, consequently, the amount of material they use will vary. Fabrics are also different. Tweeds have more give to them than closely woven wools. With experience, individual rug braiders eventually are able to determine fairly accurately how much material they need.

For a large room-size rug, however, even veteran rug braiders very often don't buy all the material they need at once. Sometimes they find they change their minds about certain colors before the rug is completed. When braided, laced and put on the floor, materials occasionally look different from the way the rug braider had visualized the finished product. Here are a few guidelines to assist you in determining the amount of fabric needed.

BY THE YARD

Barbara Fisher, of Holbrook, Massachusetts, who is well-known throughout New England for her beautiful custom-made rugs, uses slightly under a yard of material, 54 inches wide, to braid 1 square foot. Her strips are an inch and a half wide. Thus a 3 x 5 rug would take approximately 15 yards of material.

If you are planning a color-coordinated rug, and buying new material, it would be best to purchase the maximum amount. You may not be able to match the color later if the material goes out of stock. (An exception to this rule: The Dorr Mill Store and Braid-Aid listed at the end of this book, *Sources for Wool and Braiding Accessories*, maintain an open stock of colors at all times.)

BY THE POUND

If you decide to order wool by the pound, consult the chart at the end of this chapter. It gives minimum and maximum amounts of wool needed for specific rug sizes. Most rug braiders estimate they use from two-thirds to three-fourths of a pound of wool for 1 square foot of braided rug. This is after all the excess material has been trimmed off. For example, if using a man's overcoat, don't do the weighing-in until you've ripped the coat apart. Weigh only those pieces of wool that will actually go into your rug.

Allow for Waste

When purchasing wool by the pound (that is, not precut in strips for braiding) allow anywhere from 10 to 20 percent waste. For example, if you buy 10 pounds of material, you'll find that about 2 pounds will be narrow strips or uneven edges you can't use.

SCALE FOR WEIGHING

If you have a baby scale put away in the cellar or attic, get it out. It's perfect for weighing wool not only when planning the rug but when determining the correct amount of material for dyeing.

FABRIC REQUIREMENTS		
Size of Rug	*Yards*	*Pounds*
3 × 5	15	8–12
4 × 6	24	14–18
5 × 7	35	20–24
6 × 9	54	40–44
7 × 10	70	49–53
9 × 12	108	74–78

CHAPTER 6
SELECTING AND PREPARING MATERIAL

Have you ever gone through the experience of having a room redecorated only to discover in a short time that stains were coming through the wallpaper or the fresh paint was peeling? An experienced workman would quickly recognize the problem—poor preparation.

So too with rug braiding. If you are using old wool, proper selection and preparation of the material often takes more time and patience than the actual braiding and lacing. But the care you take in this first important step will save much vexation later.

FACTS ON FABRICS

When sorting out the materials for your rug, here are a few facts to remember:

1. Stiff materials, such as gabardine, are difficult to work with and produce a hard braid. If too many are used, that springiness and softness characteristic of braided rugs will be lost.
2. Loosely woven fabrics, while they often come in beautiful, vivid colors, wear out more quickly than tightly woven ones.

Multicolored braided rug does not clash but rather complements geometric pattern of tablecloth and floral design in draperies.

3. Bonded materials, jerseys and knits have too much give for a sturdy and serviceable rug.
4. It is unwise to combine cotton, linen or silk with wool. These materials wear out more quickly and their texture is different from that of wool. Cottons alone, however, are excellent for washable rugs.
5. Don't use wool that is too badly worn, for it will only shorten the life of your rug. And of course, never use wool with moth holes.
6. Most rug makers insist their finished product be pure wool and refuse to use the synthetics so plentiful on the market today. They point out that synthetics attract static and don't wear well. While it may be more difficult to limit your rug to 100 percent wool, the effort will be well worth it.

STRIPPING AND WASHING MATERIAL

When you've decided on the materials to be used, remove buttons, zippers and linings from all items and cut or tear them apart at the seams to produce as many flat pieces as possible. (And don't throw away those linings in men's suits. One thrifty needlewoman on Nantucket Island uses this fabric for braiding place mats and seat covers.) Wash the material in a mild solution of Ivory Soap and warm water. Rinse well in clear, warm water.

This step is important for several reasons. It makes for a cleaner, fresher rug and shrinks the material uniformly. Later, when cleaning the rug, you won't have the experience of some sections shrinking and producing a rippled effect. Washing also softens and thickens the fabric making it easier to fold and braid.

Some of the material may fade, and it is best to discover it now rather than later when precious time and energy have been expended on one's rug braiding. If the colors continue to run or if you don't care for the color of a certain fabric, don't discard the material. Dye it with a colorfast dye. Such dyes are guaranteed against running into other colors when the rug is cleaned. (Chapter 14, *Color Creativity with Dyes*, gives many helpful hints for successful dyeing.)

Figure 1. Matchbook cover is handy measuring guide when cutting strips for braiding.

MAKING STRIPS FOR BRAIDING

The fabric is now ready to be cut or torn into strips. Tearing is faster and more accurate. Tear the material on the straight of the fabric. Bias-cut material stretches and produces braids that do not lie flat or wear well.

Don't rip all the material at once. When folded and ready for braiding, materials, depending on their weight, will produce varied thicknesses. If possible, use fabrics of equal weight. Otherwise, cut the lighter-weight materials into wider strips. They can then be folded in such a manner that they will equalize the thickness of the other strands used for braiding.

Snip the material at the top with a scissors and then pull it apart. Fran Pratt, a rug-braiding teacher from Newport, New Hampshire, uses a matchbook cover as a handy measuring guide for this step. (See Figure 1.)

FOLDING

Make several sample widths ranging from 1½ to 2½ inches. Take one of the strips and fold each raw edge to the center of the material. Bring the folded sides together with the raw edges inside. (See Figure 2.)

If the weights of materials are uneven, the braid will be uneven. However, there is a way to remedy this. When combining materials of different weights, one can obtain equal thickness by varying the method of folding. For example, in a lightweight material, fold one or both of the raw edges beyond the center of the strip. Next, fold the strip, thus producing a strand of greater thickness. (See Figure 3.)

As mentioned previously, it is simpler to combine materials of similar weight, but if this is not possible, experiment with cutting and folding the strips until you've determined the proper width for each type of fabric you're using. Make a note of your calculations and pin them to a small sample of the material. The next time you use a fabric of similar weight, you'll know exactly how wide to cut it. If you use any of the braid aids described in Chapter 13, *Braiding Accessories,* cut the strips in the width suggested in the directions that accompany the braiders.

Another way to equalize the weights is to use filler. Merely place a slightly narrower strip of similar color inside the strand before folding it. And if you have only a small amount of material you're particularly fond of, it will go further if you cut narrow strips of the fabric and use filler.

SEWING STRIPS TOGETHER

When the width of the fabric has been determined and all the strips are cut, they are now ready to be sewn. Place two strips right sides together and stitch on the bias, since a straight seam causes bulk and will result in a lumpy rug. (See Figure 4.)

Figure 2. Fold each raw edge of strip to center of material. Bring folded sides together.

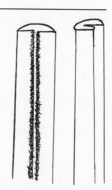

Figure 3. When using lightweight material, fold one or both raw edges beyond center of strip.

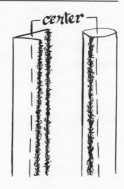

Figure 4. Place strips right sides together. Stitch on bias.

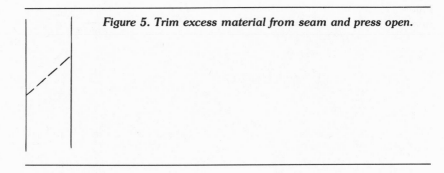

Figure 5. Trim excess material from seam and press open.

The seams may be machine or hand stitched; just make sure they are fastened securely and won't come apart later. If you join the material by hand, use a good strong backstitch. Trim excess material from the seam and press it open. (See Figure 5.) This added step will help avoid unattractive bulges in the rug.

PREPARING THE TUBES FOR BRAIDING

In one method, the strands are never more than a yard or a yard and a half in length. Longer strands are difficult to work with and become entangled with each other. In such a method, one braids and adds material to the strands as needed. The entire rug is done by alternately braiding, adding strips, and folding them as in Figure 2. If you decide on this method, hang all cut strips of the same fabric on a clothes hanger so that you'll be able to estimate quickly how much you have of any given material.

Another method is to join all the strips of one fabric together at the same time, fold them as in Figure 2 and wind the finished tube into flat rolls. (See Figure 6.) As you wind the strips, put a pin through the rolls occasionally to keep the material in place. This method is most helpful in determining a pattern and color combination for your rug. When you see the various fabrics and colors next to each other, your imagination will quickly determine the kind of

Figure 6. Wind finished tube into flat rolls.

rug best suited for your particular purposes and decor. The flat rolls also stack easily for storage on a shelf, and the material is kept well pressed. For ease in handling, make your rolls no more than 6 to 8 inches in diameter.

To keep the tubing in place so that it won't come apart while braiding and leave the raw edges of the strands exposed, there are several precautions one can take. Some rug makers iron the strands before winding them into rolls. Others insist that the open edges of the strands be stitched together to avoid frayed ends. This can be done easily and quickly by making long blind stitches about an inch in length. Merely insert the needle inside one fold of the tube and bring it up through the other fold. Repeat the process until the tube is hemmed.

Kate Forman of the New York Homemakers Cooperative Extension Service has another quick method to keep the tubing from coming apart. She winds it into a flat roll as in Figure 6, dips the roll in tepid water and then places it on a towel. When dry, the fold is securely in place.

IF YOU USE BRAID-AIDS

If you eventually decide to use the braid-aids described in Chapter 13, *Braiding Accessories*, you can eliminate many of the steps for preparing the tubing. The braid-aids are attached to the strands of material and automatically fold the raw edges and hold the strips in place as you work, thus saving a great deal of preparation time. Another advantage: They accommodate various weights of material and widths of strips so that three different weights of wool can be used in a braid with uniform results.

Since you needn't pre-fold the strands when using braid-aids, merely roll up the strips and use a large blanket pin as a reel. (See Figure 7.) Don't pierce the material with the pin, but fasten it through several thicknesses of the fabric. It will keep the wool from tangling as you braid.

Another idea: Wind the strips on a piece of elastic. (See Figure 7.) You'll have no problems with tangling.

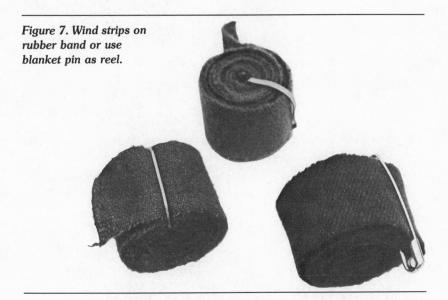

Figure 7. Wind strips on rubber band or use blanket pin as reel.

Timesaving Hint

Keep a large tote bag filled with rubber bands and strips for braiding. Take it with you wherever you go. You can easily wind up strips during P.T.A. meetings or while waiting for an appointment at the doctor's or dentist's. When others take out their crewel and needlepoint, start strip winding.

TO START BRAIDING

You are now ready to begin braiding. To help you decide whether you want narrow or wide braids, the next chapter has pros and cons on the merits and disadvantages of both. Be confident as you go into this next phase. Undoubtedly you'll develop techniques of your own as your work progresses. If the material has been properly prepared, the braiding will go quickly, and in a relatively short time you'll be the proud owner of an original and durable rug that no machine could duplicate.

CHAPTER 7
NARROW VS. WIDE BRAIDS

Perhaps nowhere does the individuality of rug braiders show up more clearly than in the width of the braids they make. If a person is impatient and likes to complete projects swiftly, the wide braids are usually the choice. If one takes the work very seriously and aims for perfection, the braids may be as narrow as half an inch. Here again, let your own tastes guide you and don't be inhibited by those who authoritatively state that the braids must be a certain width.

Betty and Reed Campbell, a husband-and-wife rug-braiding team from Allentown, Pennsylvania, believe there is a place for any width braid. They have made rugs to order for customers, and Betty has taught rug braiding. Last year they exhibited at the prestigious Jack Frost Mountain Arts and Crafts Show in White Haven, Pennsylvania.

"We took several rugs to the show." said Betty. "Some were made with wide braids and some with narrow."

The Reeds discovered that the width of the braids was strictly a matter of personal preference. Others agree. Some feel

Braided rug carries through Early American theme set by spool beds and handmade quilted coverlets.

that the narrow braids, when laced together, tend to give the rug a "too perfect" or woven look, almost as through it had been done on a machine. Others point out that very wide braids give the rug a coarse and crude appearance.

Here's a set of guidelines, pros and cons for the beginning rug braider. Keep them in mind when deciding on the width of your braids.

1. Many people find narrow braids difficult to lace together. However, if you like the look of the narrow braids but find them awkward to work with, don't become discouraged. With practice and experience, you'll soon become adept at braiding and lacing any width.

2. The smaller braid, made from strips an inch and a half wide, involves more work. It takes a great deal more braiding and a great deal more lacing.

3. If the braid is too wide, the finished rug will be bulky and may cause problems. For example, it may be impossible to open a door into the room as it will hit the rug that is too thick.

4. Wide braids give a homier, more traditional look to a rug.

5. Determine the look or effect you're trying to achieve and cut your strips accordingly. A Pennsylvania artist had a braided rug custom made by a New England craftswoman to go with the Shaker antiques she had collected over the years. When the rug arrived, she sent it back. She felt the fine narrow braids were completely out of keeping with the rustic quality of her Shaker furniture.

6. Narrow braids go particularly well with modern or contemporary furniture. When used to achieve some of the designs described in Chapter 11, *Distinctive Designs,* they are strikingly similar to rugs woven by the Indians in the southwestern United States.

7. People who have been making braided rugs for many years

often insist that the narrow braids last longer. And yet, at the Shelburne Museum outside of Burlington, Vermont, there are braided rugs made from strips 2 to 3 inches wide. These rugs are in excellent condition in spite of the heavy traffic they've been subjected to for the past twenty years.

Although simple to learn, rug braiding is a highly individual craft. Make the braid of your choice and not someone else's.

Craftspeople in New England particularly are very serious about rug braiding and pride themselves on the fine, narrow braids in their rugs. When asked about this regional perfectionism, Marie Griswold, who operates an extensive rug-braiding supply business in Pembroke, Massachusetts, and who has taught rug braiding for many years, said: "New Englanders tend to believe that if it's harder to do and takes longer, it's bound to be better."

CHAPTER 8
BRAIDING

If you've ever braided your own or someone else's hair or idly twisted strands of dune grass together at the seashore, you have already mastered the first step for making your rug. Braiding requires no great skill, but to produce a rug that is beautiful and long wearing, there are certain simple techniques that will make the difference.

STARTING THE BRAID

Take the three folded strips of fabric you've decided on for the center of your rug. Stitch two of the strips together—the same way you originally joined your material—on the bias. (See Figure 4 in Chapter 6.)

Take the third folded strip and join it at right angles to the other two, between the folds, forming a "T." (See Figure 8.) Place it near

Hit-or-miss braided rug, made entirely from recycled materials, fits in with rustic quality of paneled walls yet also looks well with contemporary pattern in bedspreads.

the spot where the first two strips were joined, but not directly on the seam. You will have less bulk and a smoother-looking start this way. Stitch the third strip to the other two by hand.

Points to Check before You Begin

Strips of Unequal Length. You don't want your rug to look bulky. For this reason it's a good idea to have the strips of unequal length. You will then be joining new material to the strands of the braid at irregularly spaced intervals. Don't have the seam joinings come together at one place in a line across the braid or there will be a noticeable bulge.

Open edges on the same side. Make sure the open edges of the folded fabric are always on the *same* side. Experts agree, it can be either side. However, in order to simplify instructions, all directions in this book are based on placing the open ends of the material to the right. It is also easier to work this way.

It is important to keep the open edges of the fabric on the same side for two reasons:

1. The open edge is laced *against* the rug and is always on the inside. In effect, it disappears as the rug takes shape. If you follow this procedure, your rug will have a more finished appearance and be truly reversible.
2. Any open edges are more likely to catch dirt, thus shortening the life of the rug. If they are hidden inside the rug, there is much less chance they will pick up soil.

ANCHOR THE BRAID

If you have no one to hold the braid for you, you can fasten it to a woodworking clamp or place it under the leg of a table. Among the braiding accessories described in Chapter 13 is a braid clamp designed specifically for this purpose.

Figure 8. To begin braid, stitch two strips together. Join third folded strip at right angles, forming a "T".

BEGIN BRAIDING

Begin braiding with either the right- or the left-hand strand, whichever is easier for you. Lay the right-hand strip over the center strip, then the left-hand strip over the center strip. Continue this way, right over center, left over center. Right over center, left over center. If you follow this method, your colors will always appear in the same order.

Be careful not to twist the strands or you will develop creases which are dirt catchers and create an unattractive braid. Remember, what you want is a nice, smooth braid. It might be well to practice braiding for a while until you achieve almost a rhythm in doing it. As you braid say to yourself, "Right over center, left over center. Right over center, left over center." It will soon become automatic. Be sure to keep the raw edges tucked out of sight as you work.

Most beginners pull the strands *down* when braiding and that results in a loose braid. (See Figure 9.) Pull the strands sharply *sideways*. (See Figure 10.) Remember, if you can get anything through the braid, such as your finger or a pencil, it's too loose. By

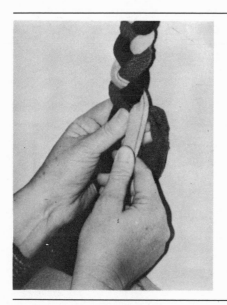

Figure 9. Pulling strands down results in a loose braid.

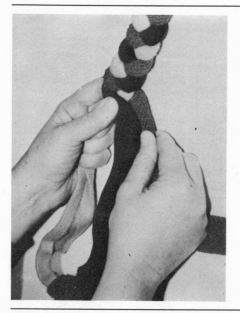

Figure 10. Pull strands of braids sharply sideways.

Figure 11. Pencil can go through braid at left which is too loose. Braid at right is firm and smooth.

crossing sharply sideways, you close the gap. The finished braid will then be firm and smooth. (See Figure 11.)

Practice braiding is most important and the little extra time it takes is well worth it. If your braiding is uneven, your rug will be lumpy. If your braiding is too loose, the rug will be limp.

Go slowly at first, perfecting your braiding. Speed will come with practice. The important thing in this first stage is making a firm braid with the strands in proper order. If the braid doesn't look right to you, take it apart and begin again. When you're satisfied with your braid, begin your rug.

OVAL RUGS

Length of Center Braid

The length of the center braid for an oval rug is determined by the size of the rug you want to make. Merely subtract the width from the length and you have the figure for your center braid. For example, a

5-foot by 3-foot oval rug would have a center braid 2 feet long. A 9 × 12 rug would have a center braid 3 feet long. If you determine the length of your center braid this way, your rug will always be nicely proportioned. (There is a slightly different method for starting a round rug or a rectangular one. It will be described later in this chapter.)

Trick for a Flat, Smooth Center

The center of an oval rug is really one long braid bent back to form two parallel braids. (See Figure 12.) Even the most experienced rug braiders often find it difficult to squeeze the first bend in a braid so that it lies flat. But there's a very simple trick for eliminating that bulky bend. All it requires is a slight variation in the braiding.

When you've braided the length needed for your center strip, stop and mentally number each strand from left to right as 1, 2 and 3. The strand farthest on the left should be on the bottom so that you won't lose your color and pattern sequence.

Step 1. Place 1 over 2, 2 over 1 and pull 3 over tightly. (See Figure 13.)

The strands are now in a different position and the colors are in a new order.

Step 2. Renumber the strands from left to right and proceed as you did before. Place 1 over 2, 2 over 1 and pull 3 over tightly. The order of colors is now back in its proper sequence. This technique is called a "modified square corner." Another way to remember it is:

1. Left over center.
2. Left over center.
3. Right over center tightly.

Repeat once more.

You now have your first curve or bend. Continue braiding in the regular manner. When not braiding, you can secure the braid

Figure 12. Center of oval rug is one long braid
bent back to form two parallel braids.

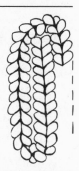

Figure 13.
Modified Square Corner.
Starting position.
Pull 1 over 2.
Pull 2 over 1.
Pull 3 over tightly.

with a spring-type clothespin to keep it from unraveling. After you
have a fairly good length of braid, you will probably want to begin
putting the rug together. This is called "lacing" and is fully described
in Chapter 9.

THE ROUND RUG

The round rug can be a disaster if you don't get the right start.
People have spent hours making such rugs only to hide them away
in a closet or an attic because the center is unattractively humped
up. They become discouraged with their new craft because no
amount of steaming or pressing will get rid of the rug's unattractive
bulge. And yet, had they known it, a very simple variation in braiding is the key to a beautifully shaped round rug that will lie perfectly
flat.

Secret of a Perfect Round Rug

In Figure 13, the modified square corner is illustrated. One uses it to curve the braid smoothly around the first bend in an oval rug. This technique is also adapted for the round rug. When you've made your "T" start, begin regular braiding as follows:

Step 1. Left over center.
> Right over center.
> Left over center.
> Stop.

Step 2. Begin your modified square corner. (See Figure 13.) Remember, if you number the strands from left to right, it's 1 over 2, 2 over 1, pull 3 over tightly.

Or, left over center, left over center, right over center tightly. Repeat this several times. Some instructors suggest you do it six times and then continue braiding in the regular way. Others do it as many as twelve times to form the center of their circle.

So much depends on how one braids, the weight of the material and the width of the strips. Experiment and see what's best for you. When you use this technique, you'll be amazed at how the braid curls itself into the proper shape for the center of your round rug. It is a much more satisfactory method than taking a straight braid and trying to twist and coil it into position.

THE RECTANGULAR RUG

While less traditional than the round or oval rug, the rectangular braided rug is particularly suitable for the modern decor found in many of today's homes and apartments. Here again there's a simple trick for achieving a neat, square corner so that the braid falls into place the way you want it.

Start the braid as you would for an oval rug and make it the desired length. Then make a sharp corner as follows:

Figure 14.
Sharp Square Corner.
Starting position.
Pull 1 over 2.
Pull 2 over 1.
Pull 1 over 2.
Pull 3 over tightly.

Step 1. Number the strands from left to right, 1, 2 and 3. Strand number 1 should be on the bottom. Braid 1 over 2, 2 over 1, 1 over 2 and pull 3 over tightly. (See Figure 14.)

Step 2. Repeat once more. This is necessary because the first turn in your rectangular rug has two sharp corners. Another way to remember this technique is:

Left over center.

Left over center.

Left over center.

Pull right over center tightly.

After making two sharp corners to turn the rug, resume regular braiding and braid up to the next corner. Lace the braid to the rug so that you will know exactly where to begin making your next corner.

After your third sharp corner, braid regularly to bridge the width of the rug, probably only a few loops. Make another sharp corner and continue braiding up to the next corner.

The entire rug is made this way—straight braiding, turning sharp corners and lacing. While many consider the rectangular rug the Ph.D. of rug braiding, Ruth Brandrup, a rug-braiding teacher in Upper Saddle River, New Jersey, thinks its success is more a matter of temperament than technique.

"If you start a loop too soon or a loop too late, the corner will not be right," she points out. "And if it isn't right, you'll have to take it out."

Her experience with students indicates that when one has braided and laced a couple of feet, a sixth sense develops about when to turn.

You have now mastered the first steps for making your rug. You've discovered the simple variations in braiding for making oval, round or rectangular rugs with smooth, flat centers. In the next chapter you'll learn how easy it is to become adept at lacing the braids together. That's all there is to it—braiding and lacing—and in a very short time, you'll see the visible results of your own creativity.

Cathedral-ceilinged foyer and beamed-ceiling living room attain sweeping unity with two oversize braided rugs.

CHAPTER 9
PUTTING THE RUG TOGETHER

U nlike many crafts, there's hardly a mistake in the rug-braiding process that can't be easily corrected if you catch it in time. Nothing is ever disastrous. The secret is in knowing *why* your rug doesn't look the way it should. In most instances, errors are due to improper lacing.

Years ago, the braids were sewn together. Although it's a lengthy and tedious process, some people still do it. However, lacing the loops of the braids together is not only faster, it produces a sturdier rug. The lacing thread is hidden in the very middle of the rug, covered by several layers of woolen material. And because it is hidden, the rug is truly reversible.

While there is no right or wrong side to a well-made rug, each side is subtly different. The top side, the one that you braid on, has a raised or scalloped look. It is brighter and almost three-dimensional in appearance. The bottom side, the one that you lace on, has a flatter appearance and lacks the depth of color of the top side.

You lace on the bottom side, clockwise, so that you always have your work in front of you. In this way, you can see what you're doing, and the body of the rug will be flat rather than hanging over

Braided mat in kitchen's work area is comfortable for standing and adds cheery note to copper-colored appliances, dark woods and tile floor.

the edge of the table. This is very important, for only when the rug is flat can you determine if it's being laced properly.

STARTING THE RUG

Oval Rug

When you first bend the braid for the center of your rug, the angles of the loops on both braids go in the same direction and can't be laced properly. So it's best to begin your rug by sewing the braids together.

Use carpet and button thread and the longest, thinnest needle you have. Start at the bend and go through the folds of the two inside loops from side to side hiding the thread. Continue sewing back and forth the length of the braid until you've gone around the second bend. Transfer the thread to a bodkin or blunt-edged lacer.

If you decide, however, to use the special lacing thread for rug braiding described in Chapter 13, *Braiding Accessories*, clip the thread and tie it off. Next, put the lacing thread through the eye of a darning needle and knot one end. Work the needle through the fold of an inside strand at the point where you've stopped sewing and will begin lacing. The knot will be hidden in the fold. Transfer the thread to a bodkin or blunt-edged lacer.

Position the braids so that the loops are not exactly side by side but slightly at an angle to each other. (See Figure 15.) Lacing is done by going under the inside loop of a braid with the lacer and bringing it up and out. The lacer should never penetrate the material. Work back and forth from one braid to another, almost like the pattern of ribbon candy. (See Figure 16.)

Draw the thread very tightly so that it is not visible between the loops. If occasionally the thread shows after lacing, tuck it under and out of sight with the tip of the lacer. Keep this rhythm in mind while lacing: Under and up, under and up, under and up, always remembering to pull the lacing thread tightly. This is called "interlocked lacing" and gives almost a woven look to the rug.

Figure 15. (left) Position braids so loops are not side by side but slightly at an angle to each other.

Figure 16. (right) Go under inside loop of braid with lacer, bringing it up and out. Go back and forth from one braid to another.

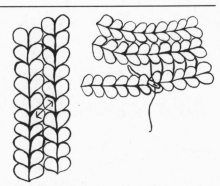

Secret of a flat rug. Each new row of the rug is larger than the previous one, anywhere from 5 to 7 inches. In order to accommodate the additional length of braid, you skip some loops on the outside braid when you're lacing. If this isn't done, the rug will buckle. Skipping a loop is always done on the *outside* braid, never on the rug itself. Remember, you are trying to ease in or accommodate the longer, outside braid to the shorter perimeter of the body of the rug.

Always skip on the curve of the rug. If done on the straight sides, the rug will ripple. When you skip a loop, mark it with a pin. In this way, you will be able to space the skips more evenly on each new row.

Also, remember that your oval rug has two curves on the top and two on the bottom. (See Figure 17.) Treat them as halves of a circle and balance the skips on all four curves. This will keep your rug uniform and symmetrical. On the other hand, if you skip in the same places as you add each row, you may find you have points in the curve.

When to skip a loop. "How can I tell when to skip a loop?" asks the beginner.

"Common sense," answers the experienced instructor.

When you've just pulled the lacing thread out of a loop on the rug (not on the braid), use this test: The thread should come straight down at an angle where the two loops of the braid being attached come together. In other words, if the next loop on the braid is ahead of the thread, lace it. (See Figure 18.) If the loop is in back of the thread, skip it. (See Figure 19.)

Round Rug

Just as there's a slight difference in the braiding technique when starting a round rug, the lacing method varies. If you've made the braid for your round rug as described in Chapter 8, it will coil naturally into the right position. (See Figure 20.) You'll find it easier to start the center by sewing the coiled braid together with lacing thread and a darning needle. Hide the stitches within the folds of the strands.

After several stitches, transfer the thread to a lacer and begin lacing. Since the round rug is a continuous curve, it is necessary to skip a great many loops on the braid being attached, particularly in the beginning. For a while, skip every other loop. Generally, this is necessary until the rug is about the size of a small luncheon plate. As the rug grows larger, fewer skips are needed.

Don't be discouraged with the shape of your rug in the beginning. It may not be too round but it will take proper form as it grows larger. Also, if the rug ruffles it's not serious. This means that you're skipping more loops than necessary. If this happens, merely go around a row or two with no skips and the rug will flatten out.

HOW TO CORRECT BUCKLING (CUPPING) OR RUFFLING

Buckling, or cupping, occurs when you don't skip enough loops. The edges of the rug turn up and do not lie flat. If this happens, unlace some of the braid until the cupping disappears. Relace, skipping loops on the outer braid as described in this chapter under *Secret of a Flat Rug.*

Ruffling is more common on round rugs, but it can happen on

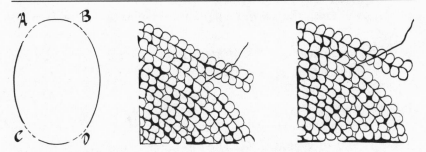

Figure 17. (left) Rug has two curves on top (A and B) and
two on bottom (C and D).

Figure 18. (center) If the next loop on the braid is ahead of
the thread, lace it.

Figure 19. (right) If the next loop on the braid is in back of
the thread, skip it.

Figure 20. Start center of round rug
by sewing coiled braid together
with lacing thread and darning
needle.

oval rugs. It occurs when you skip too many loops and produces a wavy, up-and-down edge on the rug. It is easily corrected and there is no need to take out the lacing. Simply lace one or two rows without any skips at all and the edges will flatten out.

Finishing the Rug

When your rug has reached the size you want, taper each strip from 5 to 7 inches. (See Figure 21.) The three strips should be trimmed to different lengths for a smooth and gradual finish.

Turn under the edges and blindstitch each strip with matching thread. Braid the small tubes to the end and lace to the rug as far as possible.

Sew the shortest tube under one of the others with matching thread. Wrap the two remaining tubes around each other and sew together. Work the tubes into the loops on the rug by sewing back and forth. Keep the stitches hidden.

Caution. Always work on a flat surface. If you work with the rug in your lap, you may get buckling. As the rug increases in size, you can roll up the opposite end so that you can continue working on a table. However, it is important to spread out the rug occasionally and see how the colors look with each other. Ruth Brandrup, now an experienced rug braider, made her first rug in a small area and didn't keep it open. As a result, she feels the center is wrong for the rest of the rug.

When the rug gets to be very large, you may want to put it on the floor and do your braiding and lacing there. The ends can easily be tucked underneath out of sight when you're not working on it so that if you have guests, there'll be no need to roll it up and put it away.

ADDING EACH BRAID SEPARATELY

Most rugs are made with one long continuous braid. You alternately

Figure 21. To finish rug, taper each strip five to seven inches. For smooth, gradual finish, each strip should be trimmed to a different length.

braid and lace until the entire rug is completed. This is called "spiral braiding."

However, as you advance in the craft, you may want to try another method in which each circuit of the rug is braided and laced separately. While it takes longer and is more work than spiral braiding, it gives the rug a more finished look. This procedure is also useful if you're making a very contemporary rug and want abrupt changes of strong color. It's a more formal style in contrast to the friendlier, more casual continuous braid. This technique can also be used to repair worn spots or cigarette burns in a rug.

Oval Rug

After you've sewn your center together, taper the braid as when finishing a rug. Next, make a braid long enough to go around the rug plus a few inches.

When adding each row separately, you don't begin the braid with the usual "T" start method described in Chapter 8 which hides the ends of the strands. Instead, begin the braid as follows:

1. Fold each strand lengthwise, right sides together.
2. Stitch each one across the top and down the side for about an inch. (You can do this by machine or by hand.)
3. Trim the edges and turn the sewn strands right side out.

4. String the strands on a safety pin with the open folds of the material to the right.
5. Begin braiding.

When you've braided a few inches, sew across the top of the braid to hold it in place. Use a strong, double-duty thread in matching colors. Be careful not to pull the ends together into a point. Keep them the same width as the rest of the braid. When finished you can remove the safety pin, as it is no longer needed to hold the strands in position.

Continue braiding. Lace the braid to the rug, leaving about 2 or 3 inches loose at the end. When you reach this spot, cut the ends of the strips to follow the contour of the rug and match up with the strips at the beginning of the braid.

Stitch these strands just as you did when you started the braid: Right sides together, across the top and down the side for about an inch. Trim the edges and turn the strands right side out. Braid to the end. Hold the ends in place with a safety pin. Sew across the end of the braid to hold it in place. Remove the safety pin.

With a long, thin darning needle, sew the two ends together, hiding your stitches in the loops of the rug. Be sure to do it on both sides of the rug.

Don't have one strand on top of another. The ends should dovetail or fit together so that you can hardly see the place where they join. When finished sewing, lace the remaining few inches.

Round Rug
Start the rug as described for continuous braiding. When it is about 12 inches in diameter, taper. Add each new round of braid on the remainder of the rug as described for an oval rug.

HOW TO KEEP DESIGN IN A RUG

In Chapter 11, *Distinctive Designs*, there are directions for creating design in braided rugs with the use of color. However, design can be

Figure 22. First color change is made at point A. As you continue to add new rows of braid, subsequent changes are made in each strand above point A, following path of dots.

lost on the curves of a rug when one skips loops on the outside braid to keep the rug from buckling.

Here's a simple way to keep the design intact on the curves as well as the two sides: When lacing, always skip loops in multiples of three. This is done because there are three strands in a braid. If you skip three loops on each curve, you'll always bring back the design.

Remember, these three skips are made on *each* shoulder of a curve. There will be six around one full curve. (See Figure 17. Curves A and B should each have three skips.)

HOW TO CHANGE COLOR

New colors should be introduced into a rug very subtly, otherwise you'll have a jarring, unattractive color break. Change one color at a time, high on the shoulder of a curve. Think of the curve of your rug as a clock, with the center of the curve being twelve o'clock. The first color change should come at either eleven o'clock or one o'clock. All subsequent changes should be made in a line right above the first change. (See Figure 22.)

Change only one strand in the braid at a time. In other words, it will take three complete rows to get into an entirely different color combination. You can change every single row if you want to as long as you only change one color at a time.

Now that you know the technique for changing colors skillfully, you're ready to try some of the exciting ideas with color combinations described in the next chapter. You'll discover that color serves a very definite purpose in your braided rug as you learn how to make color work for you, do what you want it to or express a mood.

CHAPTER 10
HOW TO COMBINE
COLORS EFFECTIVELY

H ow does one make a new rug look old so that it goes with antiques?

When Phoebe Dierdorff of West Linn, Oregon, first pondered this problem, she hit upon a formula of interest to all rug braiders who want a specific kind of rug for a specific purpose: *Make color work for you.*

The Dierdorff home, filled with beautiful old pieces of pine, maple and cherry, soon had a handmade braided rug that enhanced rather than detracted from the other furnishings. Beiges, tans and browns brought life and warmth to the antiques. But whether your decor is traditional or modern, skillful use of color can produce results that will give a distinctive quality to your rug.

Ruth Brandrup, of Upper Saddle River, New Jersey, who has also given demonstrations at antique shows, offers the following advice: "Throw out the window all those preconceived notions about color you might have had. Experiment. Be daring. Have fun and try combinations you never thought you would."

Braided rugs in master bedroom define separate areas for "take home" office work and mini-sitting room.

Her advice has inspired many a beginner to color-plan a rug with enthusiasm as well as confidence. And Grace Oldham of Nantucket Island, who has made many rugs for members of her family and friends, offers similar counsel.

"Don't worry about putting different colors together," she says and points out that nature mixes many colors with beautiful results.

While there's no need to be limited by rules, here are a few helpful suggestions for color balance.

DARK COLORS

A dark border will frame a rug, tie it all together. However, if too much navy, brown or black is used, the rug will have a very flat look to it. When using these solids, combine them with tweedy mixtures to give the rug character. While dark tones don't show the dirt, they do show dust.

LIGHT COLORS

If you use light colors for a border, the rug blends into the background. If used in the center, they make the rug appear larger. Light colors age gracefully and when blended with other shades, don't show the dirt conspicuously. Beiges in particular give softness to a rug and provide a good background for other colors.

BRIGHT COLORS

Be careful about using too many strong colors, or the rug will "jump out" at you. However, bold colors, when used in contrasting shades and combined with neutral or faded colors, produce very striking rugs.

BLUES AND GREENS

These colors are cool and restful and also make rooms appear larger. Most greens are quiet and will sink into the background. Strong blues will stand out sharply if used in large amounts.

REDS, ORANGES AND YELLOWS

Try these colors if you're aiming for a cheerful, warm effect. They make rooms appear smaller, cozier.

BEIGES, TANS AND BROWNS

These are the colors that bring out the beauty of maple or pine furniture. Use them, or mixtures with these colors in them, to enrich your rugs.

BEFORE YOU BEGIN

One of the most exciting things about color is that you can actually color-style a rug for the room it's going to be used in. Study the walls, draperies and furniture. Pick up one or more of the colors in the room's furnishings, and the rug will harmonize beautifully.

Sandra Cheverie, a rug-braiding teacher from Duxbury, Massachusetts, did this effectively when she had completed about two-thirds of a large hit-or-miss rug for her living room. She picked up the color in the room's sofa by putting one strand of gold in the braid. In the next row, she put two strands of gold. The third row was all gold and she continued this solid band for eight rows. She reversed this procedure to end the band, two strands of gold in a complete braid and then one strand of gold. She also finished off the rug with a gold border of four rows.

Another idea is to study the colors in the rugs you like and use them. Oriental rugs in shades of ivory, golden wheat, ruby red and rich blue can be copied effectively to produce a stunning braided rug. Take some time to study rugs in department stores and museums with an eye to color copying.

If you're still in doubt about colors, draw the rug first on paper with chalk or Magic Markers. Work out various shades and designs. You don't have to be an artist, as it only involves an oval or a circle.

Think in terms of colors that are pleasing to you. If you select a certain color, ask youself whether or not you'll find it easy to live with for a long period of time. Remember, braided rugs are extremely durable and long lasting.

Think in Terms of Warms and Cools

Ruth Brandrup stresses *value* rather than color, *per se*, with her students.

"I usually work with one strand of warm colors and one strand of cool colors. The third strand can be a nondescript anything, it doesn't matter. That way you get the balance between warm colors, cool colors and a neutral bond."

The finished result is the traditional hit-or-miss rug which is adaptable for almost any room. Another idea:

All the strong colors in one strand.

All the dull colors in another strand.

All the light colors in a third strand.

A different combination might be:

One dark strand (black, brown, dark maroon, navy)

One bright strand (bright yellow, reds, greens and blues)

One neutral strand (beiges, light grays, tweeds)

Jean Gardner of Oak Park, Illinois, has made many rugs from recycled materials with this formula. She finds it produces a rug that's bright and attractive to the eye yet doesn't clash with other colors in the room.

All of these suggestions are variations of the hit-or-miss rug and are particularly good when working with recycled materials. They are also helpful if you have a wide variety of colors but not a great selection of specific colors. Your finished rug will have a pleasant harmony about it in spite of the mixture of colors.

Observe How Colors React on Each Other

When used in a braided rug, color can change. Remember, every braid has three colors in it and is surrounded by other colors. It takes on the qualities of colors that appear both before and after it in a braided rug. For example, red and blue next to each other will give your rug a purple look. A certain shade of rust, placed next to green, takes on a bright, Christmas-red tone. Use that same shade of rust with black and it becomes a Halloween orange.

Texture of the material you're using also has something to do with the result you get. A good test is to take the wool you plan to use and put it together in a pile. If it looks good, it will look good in your rug. Eventually, experience will give you an eye for color. You'll discover also that materials of slightly different shades can be joined on one strand and will look similar once they are braided and laced.

MONOCHROMATIC RUGS

If you're using new wool or dyeing material, you might want to try making a rug with several shades of the same color. Such a rug can be striking in a modern decor. The secret here is to go from light to medium to dark. Do this several times, ending the rug with your deepest values.

HOW TO CHANGE COLORS

There's a right way and a wrong way to change colors skillfully. Chapter 9, *Putting the Rug Together*, gives simple directions on how to do this.

COLOR, KEY TO DESIGN

Besides creating a mood and enhancing the atmosphere of your home, color is the key to making interesting and unusual designs in a rug. In the next chapter you'll discover how easy it is to make distinctive and artistic patterns in your braided rug merely by putting colors together in a certain way.

CHAPTER 11
DISTINCTIVE DESIGNS

There's no great mystery about design in a braided rug; it's achieved with color. Sometimes it's done by the placement of contrasting colors within the braid itself. Or rows of braiding can relate to each other to produce certain designs. Once you're aware of how it's done, the rest is easy.

Here are some patterns that rug braiders have been using for generations. Use them alone or in combinations to give variety and interest to your rug.

ARROWHEAD

One of the oldest designs in rug making. Can be done with two rows of braids.

First Row. One contrasting color with two light colors. For example, one strand of red with two strands of beige.
Second Row. Two contrasting colors with one light color. For example, two strands of red with one strand of beige.

When laced against each other, these two rows will produce the design seen in Figure 23.

Oriental carpet has protective covering with braided runner in front of buffet serving table.

RICK-RACK

Three rows are needed for this design. Make the first two rows as in the arrowhead design. Repeat the first row.

CHAIN STITCH

Excellent for a border.

First Row. A solid, dark color. Suggest navy, black or brown.
Second Row. Three different contrasting colors that go well with each other and with the solid color in the first row.
Third Row. Repeat the second row.
Fourth Row. Repeat the first row.

FLOWER DESIGN

Particularly suitable for greens and pinks.

First Row. Medium to dark green, all three strands the same color.
Second Row. Two strands of pink, one strand of light green.
Third Row. Repeat the second row.
Fourth Row. Repeat the first row.

If the pink colors are kept together during the lacing, the pattern will give the effect of a pink-petaled flower with a light green center. Such a rug is ideal for a young girl's room or on a sun porch with white wrought-iron furniture.

DIAMOND

This geometric design will give your rug a very contemporary look. (See Figure 24.)

First Row. One contrasting color with two light colors.

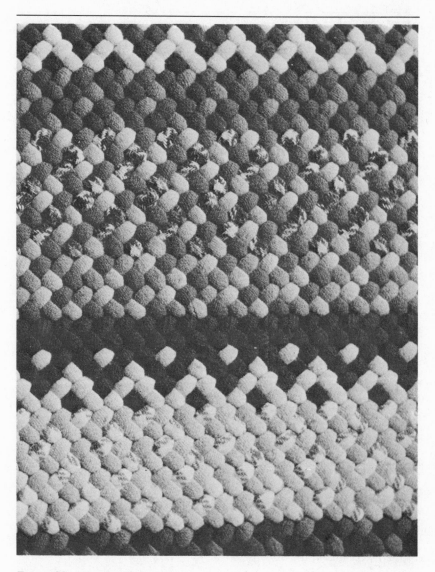

Figure 23. Arrowhead design.

Figure 24. Diamond design.

Second Row. Two contrasting colors with one light color.
Third Row. Repeat the second row.
Fourth Row. Repeat the first row.

DOUBLE DIAMOND

First Three Rows. Same as for diamond.
Fourth Row. Two contrasting colors with one light color.
Fifth Row. Repeat the fourth row.

LACY EDGE

When repeated several times in a rug, this pattern gives an overall delicate and feathery effect.

First Row. One dark color with two light colors.
Second Row. All strands should be the same as the dark color used in row one.

BEFORE YOU BEGIN LACING

For best results with design in a rug, there is a special but very simple technique during the lacing process. It is fully described in Chapter 9 under "How to Keep Design in a Rug."

Designing is part of the fun of rug making. Use these patterns alone or in combination for a unique and unusual rug. Once you begin putting different colors together, you'll undoubtedly hit upon other designs. Rug making is a craft that imposes no limits on individual creativity.

CHAPTER 12
HOW TO PERSONALIZE A RUG

Perhaps one of the most interesting ways to personalize a rug is to braid a bit of nostalgia into it. After the Civil War, women were quick to utilize their husbands' and sons' army uniforms by cutting them up for braided rugs. Years later, sitting in front of the fire, they would tell their grandchildren about the happy day when all the men came home and point with pride to the rows of braid made from a loved one's military garb.

CLOTHES CAN PERSONALIZE A RUG

Bob Gardner, of Oak Park, Illinois, feels the story of his life is woven into the braided rugs his wife Jean has made over the years. There is, for example, the suit he bought the year they were married, the overcoat he purchased when their first child was born and a variety of scarves that saw him through many a cold Midwestern winter.

Items of clothing that are no longer wearable but have special meaning can give added significance to a family rug. One woman, for many years, couldn't bear to part with a little red Eton jacket that

Sea captain's chest on Oriental rug, crewel-upholstered wing chair and oil painting of whaling voyage provide rich background for room's braided rug in pre-Revolutionary home.

each of her five sons had worn when they were three years old. She cut it up, combined it with one strand of navy and one of gray and used it for the center of a beautiful round rug in the family den.

If you have a favorite item of clothing that is no longer usable but has special memories, here's a practical way to preserve it. Work it into your braided rug. Be sure to tell the family. In years to come, they'll want to let their children know about it.

COLOR CAN BE YOUR SIGNATURE

Take your favorite color and always make certain that it has the place of honor in the center of your rugs. In this way, although each of your rugs will be unique, the centers will make all of them distinctively yours. Be sure to combine it with two other colors. A solid center will create a bull's eye and jump out at you.

Just to be different, use about a foot of a really far-out color for one strand in the braid someplace in the rug. In a large rug particularly, it won't be that obvious. But you'll know it's there and delight in its splashy look.

Here's an idea from Ruth Brandrup, who has been thinking of doing something unusual with color for years.

"Somewhere in the rug I'm working on now," she says, "I'm going to put in a band about 12 inches wide. And it's going to be a riot of color."

Designed for her classroom, the rug is basically a warm, sunny yellow with bright orange and red. No doubt the finished product will reflect her outgoing personality and enthusiasm for life. Neatly rolled up, ready to be braided for that riot of color she wants, are several strands of kelly green, purple, bright blue and the strongest orange she could find.

EXPRESS YOUR INDIVIDUALITY WITH PATTERN

Chapter 11, *Distinctive Designs*, offers step-by-step instructions for classic designs rug braiders have been using for years. Have the border in each of your rugs incorporate one of these designs or combine them in a color pattern that will be uniquely yours. Many rug braiders, through experience, hit on their own designs. Experiment a little when braiding and lacing. You may come up with something different and unusual that will be just the personal touch you're looking for.

SIGN YOUR RUG

Very few of the antique rugs in today's museums and private collections were ever signed. Don't make the mistake of the nineteenth-century rug braider. Sign your rug by using a simple embroidery outline stitch on an inconspicuous place on the rug.

Barbara Barber, who has been giving advice to sewers for years in her needlecraft shop in Larchmont, New York, suggests you use an embroidery thread.

"Yarn is soft," she points out. "It won't wear as well as a good three-strand embroidery thread."

She recommends DMC, an original French thread that has long been a traditional favorite of embroidery enthusiasts. It is available in most department stores and needlecraft shops. If you select a matching color, you'll be able to see the stitching but it won't be too obvious.

You might also want to include the date of completion and the place the rug was made. Braided rugs have a way of traveling, from north to south and coast to coast. Remember also that the braided rug is reversible. Sign it on both sides.

CHAPTER 13
BRAIDING ACCESSORIES

Most rug braiders seem to have three characteristics in common: They are creative, friendly and independent. And perhaps nowhere is this independence more evident than in their opinion of braiding accessories. Some say they can't be bothered with such gadgets. Others, like Phoebe Dierdorff of West Linn, Oregon, find the braid-aids help them to work faster.

"I made my first rug over forty years ago," she recalls. "I started out simply, using old material and folding it by hand."

As she progressed in her craft, however, Mrs. Dierdorff found that braiding accessories were a help in working more quickly. For those who are interested, this chapter offers brief descriptions of the various aids on the market and their function. Many of the items can be purchased at local department stores or needlecraft shops. If you can't find what you want, some of the firms listed at the end of the book offer a mail-order service and welcome inquiries.

BRAID-AID

A device that automatically folds the strands into tubes, thus

Large, round braided rug gives wall-to-wall look to guest bedroom.

eliminating the need for folding the strips of material by hand. There are three kinds on the market today.

Braidmaster
Set of three. Folds and holds the braiding strips, giving a firm and uniform appearance to the finished braid. Invented over twenty-five years ago by Roger Griswold, who, with his wife Marie and their family, operates an extensive needlecraft business in Pembroke, Massachusetts. For use with medium-weight fabrics cut 1½ inches wide.

Three-Way Braid-Aids
Set of three. More advanced version of the Braidmaster. An adjustable folder for various weights of fabric cut in widths from 1¼ to 1½ inches.

Vari-Folder Braid-Aids
Set of three. Most adaptable of the braid-aids. Folds nearly all weights of fabric in widths from 1¼ to 2½ inches so that three different weights of wool can be used in a braid with uniform results. These aids are not held in the fingers but dangle just below, sliding along as one braids. (See Figure 25.)

REEL AID

A handy attachment for the Vari-Folder braid-aid. Holds rolled strips up to 15 feet long and keeps them from tangling while braiding. Only one reel aid is necessary to avoid tangling. (See Figure 25.)

BRAIDKIN

A flat, curved needle or bodkin for rug lacing.

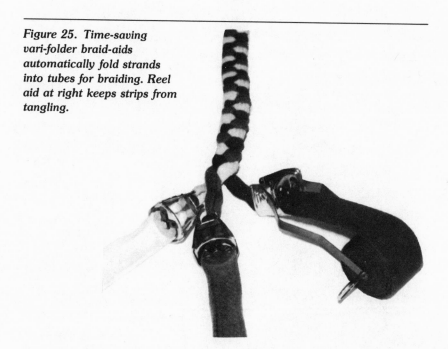

Figure 25. Time-saving vari-folder braid-aids automatically fold strands into tubes for braiding. Reel aid at right keeps strips from tangling.

BLUNT-END DARNING NEEDLE

Can also be used for lacing. Should be steel, not plastic.

BRAID HOLDER

Metal clamp for tabletop to hold the braid. Felt backing protects table. (See Figure 26.)

BRAIDING STAND

Wooden stand which holds the braid and is portable so you can move around while braiding.

Figure 26. Braid holder clamps to table top. Felt backing protects table.

RELAX & BRAID CLAMP

Portable steel braid holder that enables one to sit anywhere and braid. Clamp holds the braid firmly and is attached to a rod designed to fit the contour of the body. Can be used sitting on the floor, in a car, on a chair or a sofa.

CLOTH CUTTERS

Machines for cutting strips for braiding. Adjusts to cut uniform strips in various widths.

LACING THREADS

While ordinary carpet and buttonhole thread can be used for lacing, rug-braiding instructors often recommend a heavier thread, particularly for large rugs.

Linen Thread
A very strong thread, made for the shoe trade. Available in three-ply for scatter rugs and six-ply for larger rugs. Comes in natural or black.

Lox-Rite Lacing Thread
A tubular thread. Ends are joined together by splicing, thus eliminating all knots. Used by most professionals. Black, brown or natural.

NEEDLE-NOSE PLIERS

Perfect for tapering. When you finish a rug, use the pliers to pull the ends under the adjacent braid. Also helpful when adding each row of braid separately.

CHAPTER 14
COLOR CREATIVITY WITH DYES

There are almost as many opinions on the plus and minuses of dyeing as there are colors from which to choose. Some rug braiders become discouraged with the results of their dyeing experiments when they find the color comes off on their hands as they braid. Others have had disastrous results when they went to clean their rugs. The dyed material faded into the other material resulting in an unattractive, splotchy rug. But there's no doubt about it, we've come a long way from the days when people gathered berries to make red and blue dyes or boiled goldenrod and onion skins for yellows and browns.

Phoebe Dierdorff of West Linn, Oregon, who has been making braided rugs for over forty years, has often dyed material for special effects and finds it most satisfactory.

"If you use the right dye and do it the right way, it works," she says.

No one would agree with her more quickly than the dye manufacturers themselves. They readily discourage certain types of dyeing if they feel the consumer will be unhappy with the results. Their laboratory staffs are experimenting constantly with new fibers and

Color, size, shape and pattern differentiate three braided area rugs in contemporary Manhattan apartment.

fabric treatments. And who could resist the spectacular array of colors they offer the creative rug maker.

For satisfactory dyeing, a few simple but important rules make the difference. This chapter offers basic guidelines, and you can obtain more information by carefully following the manufacturer's package directions.

DIFFERENCE BETWEEN TINTING AND DYEING

Tinting
Tinting is applying color with a solution of the dye and hot tap water. The color does not penetrate the material completely. It can be done quickly and easily in the washing machine. It is not recommended, however, for materials used in rug braiding. People who complain that their fabrics fade, or that the dye comes off on their hands when they braid, most often use this method.

Dyeing
Dyeing is applying color in such a way that it thoroughly penetrates and saturates the material. It involves boiling and simmering the water and has produced beautiful colors and excellent results for many rug braiders. All directions and suggestions in this chapter are for dyeing rather than tinting.

PREPARATION OF MATERIAL

Always wash the material to be dyed with a solution of mild soap flakes. This will help remove any dirt, detergent, softeners or starch which might hinder effective dyeing. A thorough rinsing is also important. Don't use cold water, however, as it hardens the fibers and makes them too stiff for satisfactory braiding.

Even new material should be washed, as it may contain sizing which also lessens the effectiveness of the dyeing process. An exception to this rule is material purchased from Braid-Aid or the Dorr Mill Store listed at the end of the book.

The Cushing Dye Company manufactures a product called Plurosol which can be used instead of soap flakes. No rinsing is necessary, because Plurosol is also a dyeing aid which softens the fibers and makes them more responsive to a satisfactory dye job. Try your local needlecraft shop for this product or the notions section of your local department store. It can also be ordered by mail from most of the suppliers listed at the end of the book.

WHICH MATERIALS CAN BE DYED

Natural Fibers
Any 100 percent natural fiber such as cotton or wool takes home dyeing beautifully. However, if the material has been treated for protective purposes, this finish must be removed. Washing and rinsing will generally do this, but there are some finishes such as Scotchgard or water repellents that cannot be removed. Consequently, fabrics treated with this method cannot be dyed.

Occasionally, you'll find some threads in the fabric are a different color from the rest of the cloth after dyeing. They may be synthetic. Re-dye with an all-purpose dye.

Synthetics
If you are going to use synthetics in your rug and want to dye them, the best thing is to pretest a swatch of the material. There are hundreds of different types of synthetic fibers and weaves on the market today, and new ones are coming out constantly. Manufacturers do offer all-purpose dyes suitable for both natural and synthetic fibers, but it is still wise to test the fabric if you're not certain of its content.

Permanent-press fabrics cannot be dyed satisfactorily. Some synthetics dye beautifully but fade badly each time they're washed.

REMOVING COLOR

Dark-colored materials cannot be re-dyed a lighter shade unless the color is first removed. There are commercial color removers on the market, but they are not recommended for rug-braiding materials for several reasons:

1. Many materials today are fast-dyed. Color cannot be removed completely by any known, safe, home process.
2. Bleaching is complicated and takes a great deal of time. In some instances, it may even appear that color has been removed and then it reappears on the material after rinsing. Technicians from Knomark, Inc., which manufactures Tintex fabric dye, tell us this is caused by static electrical currents in the air on the fibers.
3. The prolonged immersion in boiling water necessary for removing color not only shrinks the material but could possibly cause fiber damage. Certainly it would weaken the fiber, and your new rug would be quite threadbare before it was even put into use.

If you have nothing but dark colors and feel you need some light shades, there is a simple home method for color removal you might want to try. Color in wool material can sometimes be partially removed or lightened by simmering (not boiling) the fabric in hot water with a little mild soap flakes and a teaspoon of ammonia for every two quarts of water. Don't use too much ammonia or it will rot the material. It is also important to stir constantly or the color will be removed unevenly.

POINTS TO REMEMBER

1. The shades you see on the manufacturer's color charts are for dyeing over white. They also show color on paper rather than fabric. Take this into consideration as you start out. If you plan to brighten beiges, grays or pastels, you will probably have to use more dye than the directions on the package suggest.
2. Dyes in the package may vary slightly from the color printed on the box, color charts or illustrated materials.

3. Dye lots manufactured at different times may vary. If possible, plan to do all dyeing of a specific color at the same time.
4. Don't crowd the fabric or it will dye unevenly.
5. If the material doesn't turn out the way you thought it would, don't be disappointed. A very dull color can take on new life when combined with two other colors in a braid. Hold the strand next to the other two colors you'll be using with it and see how it looks.
6. For best results, particularly if in doubt, swatch-test first. You can do this easily by always having a few swatches of other material in the dye bath when you're doing a large job.

EQUIPMENT FOR DYEING

Aside from the dye powder, practically everything needed for successful dyeing can probably be found right in your own kitchen.

Container
Use an enamel or stainless steel container such as a canning kettle or baby's enamel bath tub. Never use iron, aluminum or copper, because the minerals in these materials hinder the dyeing process. Manufacturers recommend that you don't dye in anything used for cooking. If it's absolutely necessary to do so, scrub the vessel out well and rinse with very hot water after using.

Stirring Rod
For stirring, use a glass rod or a large stainless steel serving spoon. Flat wooden paint mixers from the local hardware store also work well.

Plastic Gloves
Wear protective plastic or rubber gloves. If you do get some dye on your hands, wash it off with a powder-type cleanser.

Kitchen or Baby Scale

Manufacturers' directions vary. They specify that anywhere from a pound to a half pound of wool is the right amount for one package of dye. While not absolutely necessary, a kitchen or baby scale is perfect for weighing fabric not only for dyeing but also when determining amounts needed for a particular size rug.

TIPS FOR EASIER DYEING

Tear your material into strips before you dye it. Strips are easier to handle than large pieces and will dye more evenly. Tear the strips an eighth of an inch wider than needed to allow for shrinkage. To dry the material, simply put the strips on hangers.

Material should be thoroughly wet and unfolded before you immerse it in the dye. Soak in warm, not cold, water as the latter hardens the fibers and makes them resist the dye.

HOW DIFFERENT WOOLS REACT TO DYEING

Depending on the weave and thickness, wools react differently to the dyeing process. Loosely woven materials (tweeds for example) absorb dye more quickly. Closely woven fabrics absorb moisture slowly.

STEP-BY-STEP INSTRUCTIONS

1. Dissolve the necessary amount of powdered dye in a quart jar of hot water.
2. Fill a container with enough water to thoroughly cover the material you're dyeing without crowding.
3. Heat the water until it starts to simmer and add the thoroughly dissolved dye. Stir and keep the water at a simmer.
4. Put the material into the dye bath and stir. Make sure the color is evenly distributed and there are no air bubbles. Stir frequently for about 20 minutes until the material appears a shade

deeper than desired. (Colors tend to look darker when wet.)

5. After 20 minutes, if the color of the material isn't deep enough, remove it. Add more dye, making sure it's thoroughly dissolved. Repeat the dye procedure.

6. When the desired color has been obtained, remove the material and rinse it several times in water ranging in temperature from hot to tepid to cool until the water runs clear. (Sudden changes in temperature add to the possibility of shrinkage.)

7. Squeeze out the excess water very gently. Never wring or twist; it's damaging to the fibers.

8. Hang the material to dry in a cool, shaded area. It is important to do this right away or the color may come off on other parts of the fabric while slowly drying and cause spots. You can use a clothes dryer, but the material must be free of all excess dye. Otherwise the dryer may pick up and retain some color and future loads of laundry could become stained. Use a medium temperature setting.

9. If you want all the material the same shade, remove the entire batch at the same time. Fabric left in longer will come out a deeper shade.

SPECIAL EFFECTS

There are many interesting effects and textures you van achieve just by varying the dyeing process a little.

Tone Dyeing

Take several different colored pieces of material and dye them the same color. The result will be different tones or shades of one color. Such rugs are called monochromatic and can produce a quiet, restful effect in a room if soft greens or blues are used. You may not want to do an entire rug this way but can obtain interesting effects by doing several rows on different areas of the rug with tone-dyed material.

Barbara Fisher, a veteran rug braider from Holbrook, Mas-

GUIDE TO DYEING COLOR OVER COLOR

Here's a handy guide as to how colors react on each other.
Check it before you begin dyeing.

Color of Dye	Will Not Cover	Special Effects
Blue	Brown, green or deep red.	Add to bright red for purple. Add to yellow for green.
Brown	Dark greens, dark blues, dark reds or purples.	Add to green for a dull brown.
Green	Red, dark violet, dark brown or dark blue.	Green over medium brown produces olive green. Bright green over a gray and black mixture produces a nice green tweed.
Red	Green, brown, dark or navy blue or deep taupes.	Add to blue for purple. Add to brown for a reddish brown.
Purple	Green, dark browns, blues, grays or taupes.	Purple over orange produces rust.
Black	Covers all colors. However, black over brown produces a greenish tinge unless you add one-half package of navy.	Black over red gives a rusty effect. If you wish to avoid this, add a small amount of green dye.

LIGHT COLORS AND PASTELS	
Dye	*Special Effects*
Yellow	Add to red for scarlet. Add to blue for green. Add to green for a yellowish green. Add to brown for a golden brown.
Orange	Add to purple for a rust. A weak solution can tone down a strong blue that is too intense.
Pink	Add to a pastel blue for lavender. Add to a pastel yellow for a shell pink. Add to light orange for a coral.
Gold	Add to purple for brown.

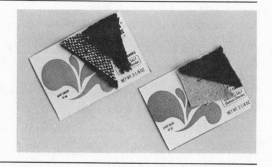

Figure 27. For future reference, staple small swatches of fabric, before and after dyeing, to front of dye box.

sachusetts, has another thrifty suggestion for tone dyeing. She uses it often for a variety of shades of green. You could adapt it for other colors as well.

1. Take some dark green material and divide it in half. Put aside one-half.
2. Take the other half. Immerse it in simmering water to which you've added a teaspoon of detergent. Simmer for about 20 minutes. This will take out some of the color. Remove and rinse. Save the water and keep it simmering.
3. If you have a piece of blue material (light or medium), put it in the colored water with a teaspoon of white vinegar. This will set the color. Simmer for about 20 minutes.

You will now have three shades of green: The original dark green, the green from which you've removed some of the color and the green you've obtained by boiling the blue material in the colored water.

Tie-Dyeing
This is probably the simplest way to obtain many different types of patterned and shaded effects.

1. Crumple, twist or gather some of the fabric.
2. Secure tightly with a rubber band, string or a pipe cleaner so that some parts of the fabric cannot absorb as much dye as others.

A simpler method is to knot the material in several places before dyeing. The tighter you tie, the sharper your pattern will be. Looser knots give a more shaded or blended look.

Dyeing is a thrifty, easy way to beautiful colors and will add another dimension to your rug-braiding skills. Be sure to keep records for future references. This can be done by stapling small swatches of the fabric, before and after dyeing, to the front of the dye box. (See Figure 27.)

There has been tremendous improvement in dyes in recent years, and the process is really quite simple. Certainly it's an easy and inexpensive way to achieve color creativity in your braided rug.

CHAPTER 15
ADAPTING THE BRAIDED RUG TO SPECIFIC DECORS AND NEEDS

What does a 1920s waterfront mansion on Long Island Sound have in common with a Manhattan apartment, a pre-Revolutionary farmhouse or a rustic lodge nestled among the pine and cypress trees of Michigan?

While it would seem unlikely that these four homes had much in common, all were found to be perfect backgrounds for that most versatile of floor coverings, the braided rug. Whether your surroundings are elegant or simple, contemporary or traditional, the hand-crafted braided rug can fulfill your decorating needs.

In this chapter are ideas for personalizing your home. Here are a few suggestions for showing off your rug at its best.

SPECIFIC ROOMS

Dining Room
Bring the rug out beyond the table and chairs so that more of the pattern will be in view. When color-planning a rug, don't forget the furniture. On page 28, chairs of bright cardinal red highlight the quiet earth colors of the room's braided rug.

Bedroom
Study your furniture arrangement and custom design your rug to

Fluffy kitten rug in shades of blue and white retains colors of nautical wallpaper but adds feminine note to young girl's bedroom.

cover those areas where there is a large expanse of bare floor, between twin beds as on page 38, or in front of a dresser as on page 42.

Living Room
The beauty of your braided rug will be shown to best advantage when heavy pieces of furniture are placed at the edges of the rug. On page 52, twin divans form a conversational grouping around the fireplace.

Kitchen
If you have a large eat-in kitchen, coordinate the room by making one rug for the dining area and another for the cooking area. Many a homemaker has also found that a small braided mat in front of the sink is most restful on the feet. (See page 54.)

SPECIAL NEEDS

One can easily see how the handmade braided rug could be a decorator's dream. There are no limitations on size or color. With such creative freedom, the homemaker soon discovers many ways to make the braided rug do what she wants it to do. Here are a few ideas. Adapt them for your own decorating needs.

Unify the Multipurpose Room
Jean and Bob Gardner of Oak Park, Illinois, often spend weekends as well as summer vacations at the family's contemporary lodge-style home in Michigan. The large master bedroom, furnished with a desk and bookcases, also doubles as a study for Bob. Two comfortable wing chairs in front of the fireplace transform the room into a quiet retreat for reading or sewing when their children entertain downstairs.

Jean has defined and separated each of these areas with one of her handmade braided rugs, and yet the overall effect is one of pleasant harmony and balance. (See page 64.)

Protect Heavily Trafficked Areas

In addition to the obvious places—doorways, in front of the fireplace—there are other locations in the home that could use added protective covering. The buffet-serving area in a dining room, for example, will wear out faster than the rest of the rug.

In the dining room of a waterfront mansion (see page 70) a rectangular braided rug provides a practical solution to this problem. It was custom designed to complement the Oriental carpet it covers.

Add Warmth to Tile Floors

Some of the beautiful domestic and imported tiles on the market today are ideal for family rooms. And no one would dispute the practicality and durability of such floor coverings. However, because this room is often on a basement level, tile can be cold in winter. Braided rugs add a note of warmth to such floors. And for TV viewing, what could be better than a small braided mat for stretching out comfortably on the floor.

Coordinate a Large Entry and Living Room

How can one retain the expansive feeling of an open, ground-level floor and yet also achieve a sense of intimacy? Faced with this decorating challenge, Jean Gardner made two oversize braided rugs, one for the foyer and one for the adjacent living room. On chilly weekends, the rugs provide additional warmth on the Indiana limestone floors. (See page 52.)

SPECIAL SITUATIONS

Will a Braided Rug Look Attractive with Other Rugs?

Naturally you're not going to throw out all your other rugs and replace them with braided rugs. Here again the adaptability of the braided rug is evident. It goes well with the hooked rug, since they represent the same era and tradition. But surprisingly enough, it is just as compatible with the Oriental. (See page 76.)

What about the Wall-to-Wall Look?

If you like the braided rug but prefer a wall-to-wall look, here's a suggestion: Measure the room's width and make a round rug with that measurement as the rug's diameter. The rug will completely cover the floor except for a few inconspicuous corner spots. (See page 80.)

THE BRAIDED RUG IN A MODERN SETTING

While the braided rug is usually identified with a traditional or Early American setting, new techniques in braiding make it well suited to the modern home. The secret is color, design and shape.

On page 86, three braided rugs cover the floors of a Manhattan apartment with off-white and tangerine walls, a chocolate-brown sofa and modern prints. The small rectangular rug to the left was made in tones of black, gray and white. In the foreground, an oval rug makes great use of the diamond and arrowhead patterns described in Chapter 11, *Distinctive Designs*. Bright reds and vivid greens in the braided runner under the coffee table are held quietly in balance with tones of brown.

Also great for modern settings are tweeds. Tone-dye a batch of them as described in Chapter 14, *Color Creativity with Dyes*. Make them up into one large or several small area rugs and then sit back and enjoy the compliments.

Large or small, round or square, multicolored or monochromatic, the braided rug has proved its versatility over and over. It can go not only from room to room but also from house to house. Don't let anyone tell you what you can or can't do with braided rugs. Instead, discover for yourself that rug braiding is a craft that will bring beauty and distinction to your home at a fraction of ordinary decorating costs.

CHAPTER 16
OTHER IDEAS WITH BRAIDS

When the nineteenth-century homemakers became caught up with rug braiding, it didn't take them long to discover that there were other ways the craft could be used to beautify the home. In many antiques shops today one finds table mats over seventy-five years old made with extremely fine silk braids. And when the New England farmer completed a handsome chair for the family home, his wife often added the finishing touch with a braided round chair seat cover.

If these women were to take a tour of some of our modern shops and department stores, they would indeed be dazzled with the fantastic array of fabrics, colors and patterns. No doubt they would soon be figuring out ways to utilize some of the scraps that so many sewers today toss aside. If you're about to embark on a do-it-yourself decorating project, here are a few ideas for giving a bright, cheery note to tired old rooms.

Historically, the most enduring quality of a braided rug has been what it represents—return to a simpler and perhaps happier way of life. Maria Mitchell House, Nantucket Island. (From Old Houses on Nantucket, *by Kenneth Duprey. Copyright © 1959, by courtesy of Architectural Book Publishing Company.)*

TEEN-AGER'S BEDROOM

Surprise your teen-ager by making bedspreads and drapes in the fabric teens love—denim. Save the scraps and make a braided rug. It can be tossed into the washing machine just like the bedspreads and drapes. Additional scraps could be used for a chair seat cover.

BATHROOM

Coordinate your bathroom with your bedroom by making the most of the beautiful patterned sheets on the market today. Use one as a shower curtain (with a plastic liner, of course) and cut up another one for the window. You'll have plenty of leftover material for a matching braided rug.

DINING ROOM

Tablecloths, particularly for a round or oval table, can be made at a fraction of the cost of a new one. Perhaps you've already tried this idea with patterned sheets but felt guilty about the amount of wasted material. Now you can use it and have braided chair seat covers to match your tablecloth.

If you're making a braided wool rug for the dining room, think about matching braided chair seat covers.

KITTEN RUG

Here's an idea that has a variety of uses, a braided kitten rug. (See page 98.) You can make it any size you want. Just be sure that the body is larger than the head.

1. Braid the head and lace as for a round rug. In the last row, make the ears by fashioning the braid into a triangle. Braid a sharp square corner for the tip of the ears.

*Single braid was often used as border in early New England
hooked rugs. In this one, circa 1860, Lucy Barnard of
Dixfield Common, Maine, immortalized her favorite horse,
Betsy. (The Metropolitan Museum of Art, Sansbury-Mills
Fund, 1961.)*

2. Braid the body. Instead of attaching the last row to the rug,
   leave several loose inches for the tail.
3. Sew the circles together at the neck. Add a colorful ribbon.
4. Use buttons for the eyes and sew them to an almond-shape
   piece of felt. Make a nose, mouth and eyebrows with felt.
5. You can make whiskers by stitching some yarn into position.

In her needlecraft shop in Pembroke, Massachusetts, Marie
Griswold has on display a blue and white kitten rug made from a
fuzzy fabric.

"Try this idea with one strand of fake fur," she suggests. "But
don't make the entire rug that way. It won't have any body."

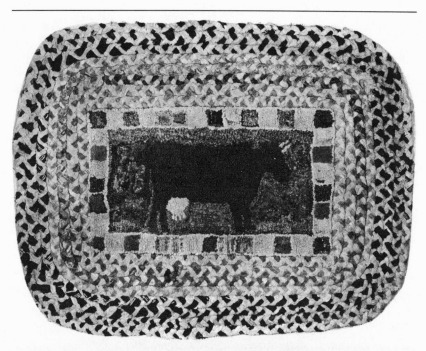

(Opposite, top) Hooked rug, featuring flight-of-fancy red cow, is well protected by several rows of thick braids. Circa 1875. (Collection of the Newark Museum.)

(Opposite, bottom) Eight-strand braid is combined with three-strand braid for border of Shaker rug made from scraps of handwoven material. (National Gallery of Art, Washington. Index of American Design.)

(Below) Border of single braid provides dash of color for shirred wool Shaker rug. (National Gallery of Art, Washington. Index of American Design.)

For a Boy's Room

Make the kitten rug in shades of brown, orange and yellow. It suddenly becomes a "tiger" sure to delight any youngster. Try it in the colors of his favorite team.

Gift Item

What new parents wouldn't be delighted with such a rug for the nursery? And if you're looking for an unusual housewarming gift, make one for your host's bathroom.

BRAIDS FOR THE HOLIDAYS

Christmas

A red, white and green mat for under the Christmas tree will last for years. And if you love those holiday poinsettia plants but hate what they do to your tabletops, braid some acrylic fabric for a protective, machine-washable table mat.

Fourth of July

Ann Killen of Nantucket has, with great results, dyed cotton jersey in earth colors for making country-kitchen place mats. Adapting this idea, one could make red, white and blue place mats for a festive Fourth of July party.

Best source of supply: Discarded men's undershirts. When cut into strips, they don't have to be folded, because the raw edges roll under by themselves.

HOW TO USE TAILORS' CUTTINGS

Your local tailor will be more than happy to fill a huge bag for you with scraps he usually throws away. Most will be synthetics and a hodgepodge of color and pattern but they can be used. Try this idea for a chair pad or a small rug for your kitchen. (See page 54.)

1. Decide on two compatible colors, like brown and beige.

2. Put all the solids, plaids and tweeds of these two colors in a large pile.
3. Separate these into three groups: Solid browns, solid beiges and patterns.
4. Begin your three-strand braid. It will be one strand of solid brown, one strand of solid beige and one strand of patterned browns and beiges.

Adapt this idea with other colors and combinations. Your finished mat will be washable and very inexpensive.

Obviously there isn't a room in the house that couldn't be made more attractive with braids. Rugs, chair seat covers and place mats can be braided in exactly the size, shape and colors you want. Table mats to go under a lamp or a vase can be color coordinated to match the rugs on the floor. And don't overlook the gift possibilities for these items, particularly for those friends who "have everything." They will be doubly appreciated, not only because they will be custom designed for the person you're giving them to, but also because they will represent your time, talent and creativity.

Nineteenth-century homemakers were not without braiding accessories. Antique strip winder was undoubtedly used by owner to prepare strands for braiding. (American Hurrah Antiques, New York City.)

CHAPTER 17
TREASURES OF YESTERYEAR

Longing for the serenity of an earlier age, Americans have often sought out the things their ancestors made and used. And whatever the harsh realities of the past may have been, the passage of time has cast a beautiful warm glow on the days of yesteryear.

The eighteenth-century New England farmer would indeed be amazed to see the prices his hand-hewn tables and chairs are commanding at auctions today. His wife would be just as astounded at the twentieth-century value of her quilts. For these items were fashioned, not with any thought for posterity, but to fulfill the immediate needs of daily life in a rugged environment.

Perhaps nowhere is the craftsmanship and thriftiness of the New Englander more evident than in the braided rugs that were created for the home. It is hard for us to imagine the great value placed on rugs in seventeenth- and eighteenth-century America. Most were imported from Europe and the Orient, and only the very wealthy could afford them. Originally, carpets were used to cover

In Nantucket Historical Association's 1800 House, braided rug enriches beauty of wide, pegged floorboards. (From Old Houses on Nantucket, *by Kenneth Duprey. Copyright © 1959, by courtesy of Architectural Book Publishing Company.)*

furniture and were found on tables and beds or hanging at windows.

In wills and inventories of Colonial America, carpets are listed as expensive treasures to be handed down to one's offspring or sold for great amounts of money. Paintings often show individuals or family groups posed around their most prized possession—an Oriental carpet. Such a painting, by John Singleton Copley, can be seen at the Wadsworth Atheneum in Hartford, Connecticut. Entitled *Mr. Jeremiah Lee* and dated 1769, it shows a richly dressed, powdered-wig gentleman with ornate buttons on his waistcoat and intricate embroidery on his vest. He stands proudly on his beautiful Oriental carpet.

In seventeenth-century England, the typical floor covering had been straw rushes, thrown on the ground to absorb dirt, grease from cooking and food scraps. During periodic cleanings, the rushes were swept up, thrown out and replaced with fresh straw. In the more affluent homes, the rushes were braided into straw mats. They are seen in paintings as early as 1635. The colonists also used such mats that were imported from the Orient. An auction notice in a 1760 issue of the *Boston Gazette* mentioned a straw floor carpet. One is also listed in an inventory of goods for George Washington. There is no evidence at hand, however, that the cloth braided rug as we know it today was ever used in Europe.

Like most crafts, rug braiding grew out of a definite need—the harsh realities of cold New England winters. Warm homemade quilts kept one cozy in bed, but what a shock in the dark, early morning hours when one stepped out on a cold, bare floor. In England, rushes had been adequate for the roughness and splinters of wood floors, but now there was a new element to contend with—freezing winters in poorly heated homes.

The colonists were here many years, however, before they could turn their attention to the thought of rugs for the home. There were more immediate and pressing needs. In an ocean crossing of a few months they had been transported from a civilized world to a virtual wilderness. They had been able to bring few possessions with them, and there were dwellings to be built, farm implements to be made and land to be cleared for the crops they would plant. The women's concern—and one that lasted many years—was how to prepare palatable meals from the strange new berries and plants they found in their adopted land.

Once adequate shelter had been provided and the larders stored with a bountiful harvest, the colonists turned their attention to clothing. Imports from England were undependable, since ships were often captured by the French. In later years, resenting the high taxes on imported goods levied by the mother country, the colonists were motivated to produce their own fabrics for clothing amd household linen. Spinning and weaving were crafts of necessity in most households. There is no evidence, however, that the colonists ever had the time or the material to make braided rugs. And yet one wonders, why is the braided rug so traditionally identified with a Colonial setting?

Philip Johnston, curator of costumes and textiles at the Wadsworth Atheneum, traces the error to Wallace Nutting. Other antiquarians agree. During the early 1900s, Nutting began collecting early American furniture and was one of the first to write a book on the subject. He also photographed many pieces of provincial furniture owned by America's foremost collectors. Because he was a forerunner in his field, errors were inevitable, as is often the case when one has no teacher. There was limited knowledge to work with and the museums of that time had little to help him. As he peered through the lens of his camera, Colonial furniture undoubtedly looked rather stark on a bare wooden floor. He remedied the situation by having his wife make braided rugs to bring warmth to the period setting.

The first documentation to pinpoint a date on braided rugs was uncovered in research done by Nina Fletcher Little for her book, *Floor Coverings in New England before 1850.**. Little says, "Braided rugs were both attractive and economical and in 1827 the Essex Agricultural Show awarded to Miss M. Locke, of Andover, for a rug of braided rags, very pretty, $2.00."

This evidence would also substantiate the fact that while the braided rug is not Colonial, its origins are certainly New England.

In all the research done for the restoration at Williamsburg, Virginia, no braided rugs were found and no mention of them was ever made in writings, wills or inventories of that area. The Virginians were more affluent than New Englanders. Most of their furniture as well as their floor coverings were imported from England. The women, caught up in the festive social life of plantation living, probably had neither the time nor inclination to make their own rugs. In addition, fewer warm clothes were needed in the temperate Southern climate, and there was not as much wool available for reworking into rugs. With less cold weather, there was also not as great a need for warm floor coverings.

One might expect to find braided rugs used by the Dutch and English in the early days of New York. But there are no available records of such rugs at the Hudson River Museum in Yonkers, New York, or in any of the Sleepy Hollow Restorations houses in New York state. Susan Dern, assistant curator for the New York State Historical Association in Cooperstown, feels that the lack of information on rug braiding in New York would indicate it was not a widespread pastime in the early days of that state.

People became very conscious of floor coverings around 1839 when, with the invention of the power loom, mass-produced carpets began to appear on the market. They were still too expensive, however, for most of the population. And so the practical homemaker, with a little ingenuity, made her own rugs.

---

*Nina Fletcher Little, *Floor Coverings in New England before 1850* (Sturbridge, Mass.: Old Sturbridge Village, page 32, 1967).

Unfortunately, braided rugs, like hooked rugs, were never signed or dated. They were made quickly and easily by the rural poor from scraps of material. It would have been difficult for the homemaker to foresee the interest in her handiwork years later. Few thought to keep these rugs when they were worn out and could no longer fulfill their function. Those that have been preserved are primarily in private collections.

While the hooked rug was also the poor man's rug of the nineteenth century, it required greater skill and artistry than the braided rug and was more apt to be saved and treasured. It was not as sturdy as the braided rug, however, and for this reason was often made with a braided border to give greater strength to areas apt to wear out more quickly. Most of the nineteenth-century examples of rug braiding in museums today are of this nature.

Joel Kopp, a New York City antiques dealer and a specialist in Early American textiles and folk art, theorizes that the braided rug probably became popular around 1830, when New England mills started mass-producing wool.

"Fabric became more available and less expensive around that time," he points out. "People no longer felt the need to recycle it back into clothing for themselves."

His observation dovetails with another account in the Nina Fletcher Little book, which relates a household hint that appeared in an issue of the *Farmer's Monthly Visitor* in 1839:

"After old coats, pantaloons, etc., have been cut up for boys and are no longer capable of being converted into garments, cut them into strips and employ the leisure moments of children or domestics in sewing and braiding them for door mats."

One group that found the braided rug particularly suitable for its life-style was the Shakers. Their records indicate that carpets were permitted, but they were to be used with discretion and made plain, never more than two colors. Robert Meador, curator of the Shaker Museum in Chatham, New York, finds no difference in the

Shakers' braided rugs and those of others except for the colors used—browns, grays and beiges with an occasional red or green.

"Braided rugs were a very common rug form in New England in the nineteenth century," he says. "Shakers were world people before they converted and brought with them to their new way of life the crafts they had known before."

The Shakers were not alone in bringing this craft with them to a new life. As New Englanders joined the westward migration, the braided rug appeared in homes on the snowy windswept prairies of the Midwest and in cabins built among the tall pines of Washington and Oregon. By this time, rug braiding had evolved into a refined craft, particularly in Massachusetts and New Hampshire. The braids were narrow and there was great use of color. Intricate designs were fashioned as the homemaker now had more leisure to make a floor covering that was beautiful as well as practical. But the pioneer woman who stepped down from a covered wagon to begin anew the creation of a home had little time for such refinements. Her rugs were made from thick braids which could be finished quickly. She was far from the woolen mills of the East and had little choice of material for creating patterns and color gradations. Like her earlier ancestors, she dug into her scrap bag and the "hit-or-miss" braided rug was reborn.

Today, one can still spot these regional differences in braided rugs. Craftspeople in Massachusetts and New Hampshire take great pride in the perfection of their rugs. Most rug-braiding instructors in these two states are certified and take an examination qualifying them to teach.

Rug braiders in other parts of the country, particularly the Midwest, tend to be more casual about the craft. And while their rugs may not be as striking or as finished as those of New England, they project a warmth and friendliness typical of their origin.

In the 1920s, a new institution appeared on the American scene, the interior decorator. As a change from the elaborate, formal mansions of the wealthy, the decorators created a new look for the second or country homes of their affluent clientele—rustic Americana. Stripped wood, hanging ivy, rocking chairs and spinning wheels were featured, with the braided rug as the focal point. In the midst of pine floors, pine furniture, white curtains and white plaster walls, the braided rug was a great relief of color. Up until this period, the braided rug had never been large.

"Braided rugs were never room-size," says Paul Madden, an antiques dealer of Nantucket Island. "They were made to fulfill definite functions—beside the bed for warmth underfoot on a cold morning, in front of the hearth to catch the drippings as food was moved from the fireplace to the table, or near the door where heavy boots were wiped dry."

Mr. Madden points out that the decorators were the first to take the traditional small braided rug and say, "Let's make it larger." Thus the 9 × 12 braided rug evolved.

Close on the heels of the interior decorators were the home furnishings magazines. They popularized, on a much larger scale and among a great many more people, what the decorators had done with an exclusive, wealthy clientele.

Historically, each time the braided rug has reappeared on the American scene, it has served a definite purpose. It was an inexpensive way to cover one's floors in the 1840s when the introduction of machine-made carpets got people excited about floor coverings they couldn't afford. It provided an attractive background for the provincial furniture of the country's first antiques collectors around the turn of the century. It was a restful change for the wealthy of the 1920s from the richness and ornateness of their Oriental carpets. Today, it seems a very practical answer to the problems of recycling and fits in with the country's renewed interest in crafts.

And yet one senses, throughout each of these revivals, a common thread—a desire to turn back the clock to another age. It is this aspect of the braided rug that will probably always be its most enduring quality, an identification with origins that represent a simpler and perhaps happier way of life.

CHAPTER 18
BRAIDED RUGS OF
NANTUCKET ISLAND

Perhaps nowhere is the braided rug more in evidence today than on Nantucket Island. This little jewel, thirty miles out to sea off the coast of Massachusetts, was once the whaling capital of the world—a cosmopolitan community of great wealth, structured on the work ethic of the Quaker religion. Its picturesque, winding cobblestone streets gave testimony to its eighteenth- and early nineteenth-century prosperity. Ordinary seamen, first mates and ships' captains built houses befitting their respective stations in life—sturdy gray-shingled dwellings with roof walks where many a Nantucket wife kept watch for incoming ships. Moneyed shipowners took over Main Street, where they erected Federal and Greek Revival homes for themselves and their offspring.

With the discovery of oil in Pennsylvania, the whaling industry came to an end. Unlike its sister ports of Salem and New Bedford, Nantucket was too far removed from the mainland to share in the nation's industrial growth. It entered a period of severe economic decline and was literally frozen in time as all building came to an abrupt halt.

Braided rugs define separate cooking and eating areas of restored kitchen. Prince Gardner house, early nineteenth century. (From Old Houses on Nantucket, *by Kenneth Duprey. Copyright © 1959, by courtesy of Architectural Book Publishing Company.)*

Today, almost eight hundred of its houses and buildings are intact, standing in this century exactly as they were in the last. They are cherished by their new owners and have been lovingly restored with period furnishings. When visiting the island, one can easily understand why the braided rug is a logical choice for floor coverings in these homes.

"I share the feeling of most antiquarians that braided rugs are more Victorian than colonial,"says Kenneth Duprey, author of *Old Houses on Nantucket.* "However, they do provide a good background for the simple antiques of an earlier period."

And just as Nantucket homeowners of the twentieth century did not wish to live without the amenities of modern plumbing or electricity, they decided to bend a little when it came to floor coverings. Handmade braided rugs somehow seemed more in keeping with the warmth and coziness of days gone by than the bare floors which would probably be more authentic for a true eighteenth-century restoration.

Another reason for the Nantucket tradition of braided rugs is the heritage of the nineteenth-century whaling wives who were exceptionally skilled needlewomen. Nantucket was never a large rural community. Its inhabitants were townspeople who lived close together and were free from the farm chores of the typical New Englander. When their men were away at sea for long periods of time (sometimes as long as four years), the women busied themselves with quilting, rug making and crocheting. These duties were combined with social occasions when they gathered at each others' homes for tea and talk and brought their needlework with them. Their lives were dominated by the sea—it was their source of income, it took their men away from them and it isolated them from the mainstream of American life.

But if the women were lonely, their men were lonely too. There were long idle hours at sea, and the men busied themselves carving scrimshaw, weaving lightship baskets and braiding mats from rope for use on board ship. Rug braiding was truly a family tradition.

Even as Nantucket became more prosperous, many inhabitants continued the craft. Quaker thriftiness undoubtedly saw the braided rug as the ideal floor covering. It used up scraps of material that might otherwise be thrown away. In addition, true Quaker believers despised ostentation, and certainly the handcrafted simplicity of the braided rug was very much in tune with their religious beliefs.

Today, the adaptability of the braided rug is demonstrated many times over by the wide variety of uses it is put to on Nantucket. It is found on the wide floorboards of the Historical Association's 1800 House which was once the residence of the High Sheriff of Nantucket County. A closer inspection of the historical dwelling would indicate that early Nantucketers were not without their "braid-aids." In the borning room is a table clamp with the figure of a bird on top of it that might well have been the model for the braid clamps sold commercially today. In fact, one of the Association's curators relates that when she was a small child, she saw an elderly relative using a similar clamp to hold strips of material for braiding.

Another historic site is the home of Maria Mitchell, America's first woman astronomer, who gained international fame when she discovered a comet in 1847. Here one finds a braided rug in front of the hearth to relieve the stark simplicity of a country kitchen.

In the George C. Gardner house in the Nantucket village of 'Sconset, braided rugs fulfill a practical as well as aesthetic function. They are used to define the separate cooking and eating areas in the restored kitchen.

The wide, pegged floorboards in these houses are typical of those found in most vintage Nantucket homes. Here again the braided rug comes into its own. When used as an area rug to cover those places that are heavily trafficked, it preserved the floor while enhancing the beauty of the wood that remains exposed.

Even rooms with patterned wallpaper find the multicolored braided rug a natural complement to the decor. The dining room of the eighteenth-century house built by Richard Macy now has leaf-

In these two homes, braided rugs preserve heavily trafficked
areas while enhancing beauty of wood that remains
uncovered.

(Opposite) Dining room–kitchen of Job Macy house, 1750.

(Above) Interior of reconstructed house in style of early
1700s.

print wallpaper with hooked and braided area rugs tying the room together.

Other homes on the island indicate that the braided rug very easily made the transition from the simplicity of the early nineteenth-century dwellings to the elegance of the later classical Federal ones. In the parlor of the Bunker-Mixter-Dell house, for example, there is a large braided rug that looks very much at home in the company of a finely carved Empire sofa and a Chippendale armchair. One's introduction to the George Coffin home is a spacious entryway with a braided rug. A few more steps bring the visitor to the front parlor, where he is enveloped in the grandeur of Oriental carpets, oil paintings and an astral lamp with dangling glass prisms.

Today, the tradition of rug braiding on Nantucket continues. Ann Killen, although raised in the Quaker faith, was not born on the island. She was brought there many years ago as a bride by her Nantucket-born-and-bred husband. Their dockside home is filled with antiques, original paintings, interesting tapestries and, of course, braided rugs. All were made by Mrs. Killen with the occasional assistance of her three children.

Grace Oldham, who is now in her eighties and has been confined to her home for the past few years, still actively pursues her hobby of making braided rugs. The whale rug she made for a grandchild proved so popular that all her grandchildren soon put in orders for a similar one. Her work can also be seen in the crafts section of the Hospital Thrift Shop, and many an island visitor has returned to the mainland with one of her rugs.

Gwen Gaillard, restaurant owner, antiques dealer and author of a Nantucket cookbook, is well known for her needlecraft skills. She finds old army blankets the best source of wool for the fine narrow braids that are her signature on a rug.

Not to be outdone by the women, as he emulates the skills of the whaling seamen, is Charles Flanagan. He has made braided rugs for many of the rooms in the family's two historic houses and finds the craft therapeutic as well as practical.

To those who know Nantucket well, it is not surprising that the braided rug is still one of the most popular floor coverings there. Unlike most communities in America, the island has managed to maintain many of the traditions of an early age. There are scrimshaw artists, cabinetmakers and fishermen earning their livelihood much as their ancestors did over a century ago. And while holding on to the skills of days gone by, the Nantucket woman has seen the cycle of rug braiding come full circle. Through the years, she resisted the wall-to-wall carpeting and synthetic shag rugs that were so appealing to her mainland sisters. Today she is hailed as the epitome of modernity as she recycles materials, participates in the nation's crafts boom and brings warmth and comfort to her home with a simplicity that has almost disappeared from the American scene.

CHAPTER 19
EASY CARE OF BRAIDED RUGS

PROFESSIONAL VS. HOME CLEANING

When you have finished one or several braided rugs, the question will inevitably arise, "Can I send my braided rug out to be cleaned professionally?"

A coast-to-coast poll of experienced rug braiders produced the following answers: 50 percent said yes, 50 percent said no. Some of their comments, pro and con, may be helpful in evaluating the best cleaning method for your rug.

"I would never send mine out to a cleaner," says Phoebe Dierdorff of West Linn, Oregon. "They might get them out of shape."

Ann Killen of Nantucket agrees with her.

"Dry cleaning kills rugs," she claims.

However, Marie Griswold of Pembroke, Massachusetts, who has made many braided rugs, insists they can be cleaned. "It's relatively inexpensive, too," she points out. "And they come back looking beautiful."

Ruth Brandrup of Upper Saddle River, New Jersey, also sends her rugs out.

Room with patterned wallpaper finds multicolored braided rug natural complement to decor. Richard Macy House, early eighteenth century.

"Tell the cleaners to treat them like any good wool carpeting," she advises. "The only thing they shouldn't do with them is hang them on a rack or a line."

This is the one piece of advice that comes through consistently: Never hang or beat a braided rug. It weakens the lacing thread and will shorten the life of the rug.

WEEKLY AND SEASONAL CARE

Like any good wool carpeting, braided rugs should be vacuumed periodically. Your braided rug is, of course, reversible. When you turn it over, vacuum it on both sides with the upholstery attachment. Move the vacuum along the braids rather than across them. There will be less strain on the lacing thread this way.

As an added precaution, Betty Campbell of Allentown, Pennsylvania, sprays her rugs with a mothproofing solution as soon as she's finished one.

CARE OF COTTON RUGS

Small cotton rugs and mats can be thrown in the washing machine. However, don't be alarmed if they come out looking very strange. They may have a bump in the center. If so, put weights on them. Or you can place them on the floor and walk on them repeatedly until they're flat and then let them dry.

STORING BRAIDED RUGS

Braided rugs should never, never be folded. It puts a strain on the fibers and may produce a crease that you'll never be able to get rid of. Always roll a braided rug, even if you're only putting it away for a short period of time. When taken out of storage, braided rugs will sometimes curl up around the edges. Merely weight them down with some books for a few days and they'll flatten out nicely.

If it is put away for a long period of time, the rug should be wrapped in an old sheet. Do not use an airtight plastic bag. The rug may rot or mildew. Remember, wool is a natural fiber and needs to breathe.

REPAIR

If the edges of your braided rug wear out, you can merely remove a row or two of braid and replace it with a new border. For worn spots or cigarette burns, remove the section, replace the wool and re-braid. Refer to the directions in Chapter 9 under "Adding Each Braid Separately." Your rug will be as good as new.

IF YOU SEND YOUR RUG OUT

Make sure you are dealing with a reputable cleaner. Too much time has gone into your braided rug to have it ruined by careless cleaning methods. If you have any doubts, check with the textile section of your local museum and ask where they have their rugs cleaned. It may be expensive but you can be sure the rug will be handled carefully.

IF YOU CLEAN IT YOURSELF

Commercial rug-cleaning products do a good job. You can hand scrub or use an electric shampooer. Also, a mild solution of detergent and water, rubbed very lightly over the surface, brightens up the rug. Caution: Don't get the rug too wet. You only need to clean the surface.

Barbara Fisher of Holbrook, Massachusetts, finds a mild solution of clear ammonia and water a good cleaner. (Do not mix ammonia with soap.) Others point out that the dry method of cleaning with an absorbent powder is better. Frequent use of the wet method will leave a residue, because it is impossible to thoroughly rinse a carpet on the floor.

Stain Removal

Speed is the best guarantee for successful stain removal. If left too long, stains can become permanent. Two excellent formulas for treating spots and spills are: (1) An ordinary bottle of dry-cleaning fluid and (2) a solution of 1 teaspoon of mild detergent and 1 teaspoon of white vinegar in a quart of warm water.

Cleaning Method

Wipe up as much as possible of the stain with a cloth. Take a toothbrush, dip it in the solution and rub back and forth very fast and very lightly so that it won't saturate the wool. Rinse with clear water. Place a towel on the area to absorb excess moisture.

For more specific directions, consult the handy checklist for stain removal below.

CHECKLIST FOR STAIN REMOVAL	
Stain	*Cleaning Method*
Acid	Detergent-vinegar solution.
Alcoholic Beverages	Detergent-vinegar solution followed by cleaning fluid.
Blood	Cold water followed by detergent-vinegar solution.
Butter	Cleaning fluid.
Candy	Scrape off as much as possible. Finish job with detergent-vinegar solution.
Chewing Gum	Ice rubbed over gum when it is relatively fresh makes it brittle and fairly easy to remove with a spatula or putty knife. If any gum remains, try cleaning fluid.
Chocolate	Use detergent-vinegar solution followed by cleaning fluid.

Stain	Cleaning Method
Coffee	Detergent-vinegar solution.
Crayon	Scrape and vacuum. Follow with detergent-vinegar solution and cleaning fluid.
Egg	Remove as much as possible with cold water. Follow with detergent-vinegar solution.
Fruit and Juices	Detergent-vinegar solution.
Furniture Polish	Detergent-vinegar solution followed by cleaning fluid.
Glue	Full-strength denatured or rubbing alcohol.
Gravy	Detergent-vinegar solution followed by cleaning fluid.
Grease	Scrape and vacuum. Follow with cleaning fluid.
Ice Cream	Detergent-vinegar solution followed by cleaning fluid.
Iodine	Alcohol.
Lipstick	Detergent-vinegar solution followed by cleaning fluid.
Milk	Cold water followed by detergent-vinegar solution. If necessary use cleaning fluid.
Mud	Detergent-vinegar solution.
Mustard	Detergent-vinegar solution.
Oils	Cleaning fluid.
Perfume	Detergent-vinegar solution and cleaning fluid.
Salad Dressing	Detergent-vinegar solution and cleaning fluid.
Sauces	Detergent-vinegar solution and cleaning fluid.
Shoe Polish	Scrape and vacuum. Follow with detergent-vinegar solution and cleaning fluid.
Soft Drinks	Detergent-vinegar solution.
Tea	Detergent-vinegar solution.
Wax	Scrape and vacuum. Follow with cleaning fluid.

CHAPTER 20
TURNING A HOBBY INTO PROFIT

There's hardly a skill that isn't salable one way or another, and rug braiding is no exception. Interestingly enough, however, most women with needlecraft skills who made their hobby profitable were never really in it for the money.

"You start with the love of doing it," says Pat Headen, who owns and operates a Stretch 'n Sew shop and school in Hartsdale, New York. "And whether it's rug braiding, needlepoint or sewing, craftspeople have two things in common: they're creative types and they enjoy doing what they're doing."

Her observations are indeed backed up by the accomplishments of people whose creativity and enthusiasm for their craft provided the basis of their success. These are the magic ingredients. If you have them, your potential is unlimited.

Like any success story, however, there are practical considerations and many questions. "How can I set a price on my work?" asks the woman whose friends are requesting she do custom rugs for them. "What's the best way to make myself known?" queries the rug braider who wishes to expand her clientele. "I think I'd be a

Simplicity of room-size braided rug counterpoints Empire
sofa and Chippendale chair in Bunker-Mixter-Dell house.
(From Old Houses on Nantucket, *by Kenneth Duprey.*
Copyright © 1959, by courtesy of Architectural Book
Publishing Company.)

133

good teacher," states another woman, "if only I knew how to get started."

If you feel your craft has reached a point where it might be financially remunerative, here are a few practical suggestions. Some, or all of them, may show you the way to expanding a pleasant hobby into a mini-career that pays cash dividends.

TEACHING

Scratch the surface of a successful crafts business and you'll usually find an ex-teacher at the helm. Teaching is also one of the best ways to become an expert in the field. For while teachers are constantly instructing others, they are also learning from students' mistakes and problems. It's a continuing education process.

If you feel you've reached the point where you'd like to pass your know-how on to others, here are some ideas for getting started.

Promote Yourself
Contact your local P.T.A., church guilds and women's clubs. Tell them about your craft. Show them some of your rugs and let them know of your availability for lecturing. Such talks can be very simple. Tell the audience how you became interested in the craft, how simple it is and how inexpensive to get started. Be sure to have a few samples of your work with you.

When you've finished speaking, invite your listeners to come up and ask questions on a person-to-person basis. Take the names and addresses of those who seem especially interested and you'll soon have a nice little nucleus of students for private instructions.

Practicalities of Home Instruction
If you decide to start out with a few students in your home, the classes will probably be small and informal. Pat Headen, the successful businesswoman quoted at the beginning of this chapter, started in her basement with a class of twenty-five.

"I whitewashed the walls, had some new lighting installed and added a few plants for a warm, friendly atmosphere," she said in describing her first classroom. Reports of her classes spread by word of mouth, and in a year the demand for her specialized sewing technique was such that she opened her own shop.

Ruth Brandrup, a rug-braiding instructor from Upper Saddle River, New Jersey, also has a special room set aside for her teaching. The studio is spacious and cheerful with a large table in the center for braiding and lacing. The tile floor has braided scatter rugs of various sizes and shapes including one with visible evidence of rug braiding "don'ts" for the students' benefit.

An old barn, refurbished, heated and then connected to the house became the studio for Barbara Fisher in Holbrook, Massachusetts, when the demands for her teaching services grew. She started out, however, correcting other people's mistakes.

"So many rugs were put away because they had bumps and bulges and the women didn't know how to fix them," she said. "When they brought them to me they were so happy with the results that they asked for more instruction. I soon found I had graduated from being a fix-it lady to a full fledged instructor."

Structuring your course. It will be easier for you and give you more confidence in your ability if you sit down and write out a lesson plan before your classes start. Decide on the number of sessions, anywhere from six to ten.

Lesson 1. Have some strips of material ready for each student. Show them how to make a "T" start and prepare the strands for braiding. For homework tell them to bring strips, washed and prefolded, and a "T" start, ready for braiding, to the next class.

Lesson 2. Show them the correct and incorrect way to braid. Demonstrate the modified square corner for making that first bend in an oval rug. Discuss the technique for round rugs with a guaranteed flat center. Show samples of narrow and wide braids. Tell them how to put colors together. For homework, have the class bring in several feet of braid in the colors and materials they've selected for their rug.

Lesson 3. As lacing seems to be the downfall of most beginners, it might be well to spend an entire class on this aspect of rug braiding. Show them how to change colors, how to skip loops on the curves. Have samples of the various lacing threads on the market.

Lesson 4. Have a lesson on braiding accessories. Midway is a good point to bring them in. Students will have mastered the braiding and lacing techniques and be more at home with the craft.

Lesson 5. Dyeing. Do some actual dyeing in the classroom. Also show the students some fabric with before-and-after results. Point out how colors react on each other and how various fabrics take dyes differently.

Lesson 6. Spend a lesson on pattern and design. Throughout the course, students should be working on a rug or a chair seat cover. Each lesson, therefore, can implement some new technique into the item they're making.

Lesson 7. While they're working on their rug, have a catchall lecture on interior decorating and the history of the braided rug. Stress the uniqueness and tradition of the craft as well as the braided rug's versatility for any decor.

Lesson 8. Describe the difference between continuous braiding and adding each braid separately. Show how to do the latter. Also demonstrate the proper method for finishing off a rug with a tapered ending.

Lessons 9 and 10. Cover ideas for personalizing a rug, care of braided rugs and how to estimate the amount of wool needed. If you're near a place that carries bulk wool, take a field trip with your students. Show them what to look for when purchasing wool by the pound.

Enlarge your horizons. Once you're giving private instructions, you have the components for a good newspaper story. Call the women's page editor of your local paper. Invite her to one of your informal classes and suggest she bring a photographer.

When you've been teaching for a while and when your publicity appears, you can take another step forward—Adult Education Programs. Compose a letter listing your qualifications and expressing your interest in teaching. Send it, along with newspaper stories about your craft, to the continuing education programs of high schools in your area. Let the local Y's know of your abilities also.

Adult Education

The woman who teaches in adult education classes will generally do much better financially than the instructor who gives private lessons in the home. On the negative side, these classes are often quite large. Sometimes there are as many as sixty or seventy students. The congenial atmosphere of a home studio is certainly quite a contrast to the large impersonal classrooms of a Y or a high school.

Many craftspeople, however, have easily adapted to this way of teaching. Personal instruction, of course, is impossible, but good lectures can be given and students can learn. The secret is to give instructions, have the students take notes and then direct them to put into practice what they've learned. Each class builds on the previous one with a final goal of a finished braided rug.

For audiovisual aids, you can make your own flip charts with white poster board and Magic Marker. Show the main steps in diagram form. In these large classes it's especially important to stress the reason behind each step. Students must know the *why* of what they're doing so that the technique will follow naturally.

What to Charge

Fees for adult education courses are usually predetermined. Most often you will receive a certain amount per course for each student in the class. For home lessons, it's almost up to the individual to determine what his or her own time is worth. Decide what you feel you should be making per hour and prorate it among your students.

Hints from Experienced Teachers

Collect your fees in advance. Let them know that it's a flat price whether they appear for one lesson or ten. Too often, if the money is collected at each session, students come for the first week, get started and then disappear. The instructor won't see them again until they have a rug with trouble. They'll often spend an entire afternoon having you correct their mistakes, with no fee of course.

Be aware of the desire for instant success. Most people want immediate and perfect results. When your students do well, praise them. Try to make them realize that mistakes are part of the learning process. Also, not everyone masters the skill at the same speed. Encourage those who are slower.

Prepare yourself for a wide variety of personality types. If you're teaching during the day, your typical student will most often be the homemaker who has no desire to return to work or school and enjoys crafts. Her home and her family are very important to her. This type is usually relaxed, congenial and very similar in temperament and interests to the person who teaches crafts.

In the evening, however, your students will frequently be working women. Many times they bring with them the tensions and frustrations of an office or an unhappy career situation. Another group that attends evening classes are young mothers who must rely on their husbands to do baby-sitting. Often, these young women feel the need for a night out which they justify by learning a practical, money-saving craft.

CUSTOM WORK

How to Get Started

Interior decorators. These firms are always looking for a source that supplies something unusual expertly crafted. Virginia Cheney, a New York–based interior decorator, suggests you contact those in your area.

"Tell them you can make braided rugs to special order, special sizes and special colors," she advises. "They may not have an immediate prospect for your work but they will be happy to have you as a source for future possibilities."

Rug manufacturers' representative. When interior decorators are looking for a special-order rug, these are the firms they contact. The manufacturers' representative has access to a broader range of clients than the decorator. For the most part they are dealing with individuals willing to spend large amounts of money for custom work. Ask an interior decorator for help in pinpointing these firms.

Craft fairs. Many a craftsperson was introduced to potential buyers via local craft fairs. Watch for notices of these fairs. Check craft magazines and newspapers. Ask the crafts editor of your local paper about any groups in your community.

You might get your own groups together for a show. Booths featuring quilts, hooked rugs and needlepoint items would be a natural complement to braided rugs. Include a furniture maker and have that person construct your displays.

When people seem interested in your work, take down their names and addresses. Send mailers to them about your next show or about any new aspect of your business.

Antiques dealers. Most collectors who live with their antiques would like antique rugs. However, very few of the rugs of an earlier period have survived. Those that do turn up are usually too fragile for daily use. The braided rug complements antique furniture beautifully. Visit your local antiques dealers. Show them samples of your work. Attend antiques shows. Dealers may have clients who would be interested in a custom-order braided rug.

Fund-raising events. Offer one of your rugs as a prize for a local fund-raising or charitable event. It's a quick way of getting exposure and could lead to an interesting article about you in the local press.

Newspaper publicity. Use ecology as a news peg and call the women's page editor of your paper. Tell her you're involved in a craft that uses recycled materials and produces warm, cozy rugs for pennies. Invite her to your home so she can see for herself the results of your handicraft.

Selling on consignment. Many craftspeople have successfully sold their work on consignment with boutiques, craft shops or the women's exchange establishments found in many communities. In this arrangement, a set price for the rug is agreed upon. When it's sold, you receive a percentage of the selling price.

Claire Freeman, a rug-weaving instructor at the Westchester Arts Workshop in White Plains, New York, offers this caution about consignment.

"If a shop takes things on consignment, they may treat them carelessly. If the merchandise doesn't sell, it's no loss to them as they've made no financial commitment."

She points out that some owners will buy the rug outright, but you won't get as much.

"They don't want to pay what the merchandise is worth," she says, "because there is always the possibility they'll get stuck with it."

Word-of-mouth advertising. Most rug braiders who are successful in the custom-work field agree: There is no substitute for word-of-mouth advertising. Let everyone know you are interested in selling your rugs. Feel your way until you develop a reputation. One sale often leads to another as people become aware of your work.

What to Charge
The monetary value a craftsperson places on his or her finished

work has to be a very personal thing. What is your time worth per hour? Are you willing to charge less because you work at home and don't have the overhead of running a business?

Barbara Fisher charges a set price per square foot for anything except very unusual rugs like a cloverleaf or hexagonal shape. She knows from experience how long it takes her to complete one square foot of rug and how much material she will need. As the price of wool fluctuates, she adjusts her prices accordingly.

How to Deal with Clients

Make your customers aware of the fact that they are truly getting a one-of-a-kind handcrafted rug. Your own home can be your showroom and probably provides the best setting for displaying your handiwork. Discuss size, design and color. Order a wool color chart from the Dorr Mill Store referred to in Chapter 21. Tell the clients that since they are going to live with their rugs, they have the option of selecting the colors they are most comfortable with. Generally they will let you decide how to put the colors together.

Reread the section in Chapter 4 on the various types of wool and be knowledgeable about the subject. Advise your customers that only the best materials will be used and that they will not be shortchanged with inferior quality.

CHAPTER 21
SOURCES FOR WOOL
AND BRAIDING ACCESSORIES

SOURCES FOR RUG BRAIDING ACCESSORIES

California
Some Place, 2990 Adeline Street, Berkeley, CA, 94703. Phone: (415) 841-6716. Sells rug-braiding supplies retail, wholesale and mail order. Retail sales in showroom open Tuesday, Friday and Saturday from 1:00 to 5:30 P.M. Write for catalog.

Connecticut
Harry M. Fraser Company, 192 Hartford Road, Manchest, CT, 06040. Phone: (203) 649-2304. Rug braiding suppliesa and material. Instructions available.

J's Shop, Litchfield Road, Norfolk, CT 06058. Phone: (203) 542-5216. Rug-braiding supplies and material. Instructions available.

Maine
Berry's of Maine, 20-22 Main St., Yarmouth, ME 04096. Phone: (207) 846-4112. Rug-braiding supplies. Reatil and mail order. Catalog available upon request.

Braided rug in foyer looks very much at home with elegant furniture of adjacent parlor. George Coffin House, 1820. (From Old Houses on Nantucket, *by Kenneth Duprey. Copyright © 1959, by courtesy of Architectural Book Publishing Company.)*

Maryland
Golden Fleece, New Market, MD 21774. Phone: (301) 865-5440. Brading supplies and materials. Instructions available. Write for brochure with map giving directions from nearby Baltimore or Washington, D.C.

Massachusetts
Braid-Aid, 466 Washington Street, Pembroke, MA 02359. Phone: (617) 826-6091. Carries a complete line of accessories and materials for rug braiding and allied crafts. Retail shop. Mail order. Instructions available. Offers discounts to shops and teachers. Send for latest catalog, enclosing one dollar.

Michigan
Carey Mission Ruggery, 206 Philip Road, Niles, MI 49120. Phone: (616) 683-8881. Hooking and braiding supplies. Sells clean, used wool, forty cents for a skirt, one dollar for a coat. Always an excellent supply of mixes. Instructions available. Open Wednesdays from 9:00 to 9:00 or by appointment.

Minnesota
Lavonne Swanson, 2924 Sumter Ave. N., Minneapolis, MN 55427. Phone: (612) 544-5419. Braiding supplies. Offers instruction at a learning center and in the school district's Community Education program.

New Hampshire
Dorr Mill Store, Guild, NH 03754. Phone: (603) 863-1197. Supplies, patterns and kits for rug hooking and braiding. Instructions available. Send for price list.

New Jersey
Constructive Arts & Crafts Corporation, Spotswood Shopping Center, Spotswood, NJ 08884. Phone: (201) 251-1800. Rug-braiding accessories. Catalog available.

Ruth Brandrup, 70 Knollwood Road, Upper Saddle River, NJ 07458. Phone: (201) 327-9564. Supplies and instruction. Send self-addressed stamped envelope for further information.

Ohio
The Rug House, Pat Nolan, 1437 Herschel Avenue, Cincinnati, OH 45208. Phone: (513) 871-0890. Rug-braiding accessories, new wool and instructions.

Pennsylvania
The Amish Farm and House, 2395 Lincoln Highway East, Lancaster, PA 17602. Phone: (717) 394-6185. Rug-braiding supplies retail and mail order. Instructions available. Catalog sent upon request.

Virginia
Joan Sealey, 6820 Barnack Drive, Springfield, VA 22152. Phone: (703) 451-6528. Rug-braiding supplies, new wool and instructions.

GOOD BUYS ON NEW WOOL

Prices quoted were in effect when this book went to press.

California
Levine Brothers, 530 S. Los Angeles Street, Los Angeles, CA 90013. Phone: (213) 624-6541. Wool remnants always available.

Connecticut
Harry M. Fraser Company, 192 Hartford Road, Manchester, CT 06040. Phone: (203) 649-2304. Sells wool remnants by the piece and by the pound. Also sells by the yard from bolts.

J's Shop, Litchfield Road, Norfolk, CT 06058. Phone: (203) 542-5216. Sells precut wool strips for braiding. Wide variety of colors available.

Illinois
Northwest Fabrics, 4030 High School Road, Indianapolis, IN 46234. Phone: (317) 299-6174. Wool remnants available during most of fall and winter months.

Indiana
Northwest Fabrics, 4030 High School Road, Indianapolis, IN 46-234. Phone: (317) 299-6174. Wool remnants available during most of fall and winter months.

Iowa
Northwest Fabrics, 2740 Douglas Road, Des Moines, IA 50310. Phone: (515) 274 - 0784. Wool remnants available during most fall and winter months.

Maine
Oxford Mill End Store, Oxford, ME 04270. Phone: (207) 539-4451. Rug strips, thirty cents a pound. Pieces less than a yard, fifty cents a pound. Remnants one yard and over, a dollar a yard. Most of the material is coat weight. Usually have wide color selection.

Maryland
Golden Fleece, New Market, MD 21774. Phone: (301) 865-5440. Largest stock of woolens in Maryland. Sells remnants by the pound and by the yard. Also material from the bolt. Wide selection of weights and colors available at all times. Write for brochure with map giving directions from nearby Baltimore or Washington, D.C.

Massachusetts
Braid-Aid, 466 Washington Street, Pembroke, MA 02359. Phone: (617) 826-6091. Carries coat-weight and medium-weight wool by the yard or in precut 15-foot strips. Wide selection of colors. Also sells wool by the pound. Retail. Mail order. Has shipped material as far north as Alaska and as far west as Hawaii.

If you're visiting Cape Cod or Boston, it will be well worth your while to stop by here. For further information about prices and ordering wool by mail, write for latest catalog, enclosing check or money order for one dollar.

Clement Textiles, Incorporated, Kneeland Street, Boston, MA 02117. Phone: (617) 542-9511. Sells pieces 1½ yards long, 60 inches wide at low prices. Variety of colors available. Does not have these buys every day, so check before going.

Eastern Textile Corporation, Kneeland Street, Boston, MA 02117. Phone: (617) 426-4500. Sells seconds 60 inches wide at half price. Has wide variety of colors.

Minnesota
Lyman's, 110 N. 5th Street, Minneapolis, MN 55401. Phone: (612) 332-8215. Sells wool remnants in large plastic bags. Call ahead to find out what's available. Ask for Fred Raidin.

The Wool-n-Shop, 101 27th Avenue, S.E., Minneapolis, MN 55414. Phone: (612) 331-1813. Affiliated with the Northwest Wool Marketing Corporation. Good buys on wool by the yard.

Missouri
Slabotsky & Sons Tailors, 1102 Grand, Kansas City, MO 64106. Phone: (816) 842-3445. Good buys on wool in short lengths and by the yard.

Montana
Northwest Fabrics, 4800 10th Avenue, S., Great Falls, MT 59405. Phone: (406) 761-4773. Wool remnants available during most of the fall and winter months.

Nebraska
Northwest Fabrics, 8260 Grover, Omaha, NB 68144. Phone: (402) 393-7675. Wool remnants available during most of the fall and winter months.

New Hampshire
Dorr Mill Store, Guild, NH 03754. Phone: (603) 863-1197. The Cadillacs of wools, woven especially for rug hooking and braiding, come from this mill. Sixty colors maintained in open stock at all times. Width, 57 inches. Mail order. Retail. Write for price list.

Does not sell wool by the pound by mail. However, if you are in New Hampshire's Dartmouth–Lake Sunapee area, don't miss the fantastic buys in bulk wool at this store. Has large plastic bags filled with remnants at fifty cents a bag. Also sells yard-and-a-half remnants for a dollar a pound.

New York
David Satran, 81 Green Street, New York, NY 10012. Phone: (212) 226-0279. Sells bulk wool by the yard. Wide selection. Call before going to make sure owner is at the warehouse. Mail order. For samples and prices, send fifty cents in coin or stamps.

North Dakota
Northwest Fabrics, 2015 Library Circle, Grand Forks, ND 58201. Phone: (701) 772-1500. Wool remnants available during most of the fall and winter months.

Ohio
The Rug House, Pat Nolan, 1437 Herschel Avenue, Cincinnati, OH 45208. Phone: (513) 871-0890. Carries wool by the pound, by the yard, remnants, ends of bolts. Selection varies depending on shipments from suppliers. Call beforehand.

Oregon
Fern Carter, 1524 Southeast Poplar Road, Portland, OR 97214. Phone: (503) 235-5254. Sells wool at $3 per pound, certain colors $4 per pound. Lengths vary, anywhere from three to ten yard pieces.

Pennsylvania
The Amish Farm & House, 2395 Lincoln Highway East, Lancaster, PA 17602. Located in the heart of the Pennsylvania Dutch country, the Amish Farm & House is a working replica of an Old Order Amish farmstead. Its shops, offering many hand-crafted items, also sell half-yard wool remnants by the pounds. Another thrifty buy for rug braders is wool strips, about two inches wide, by the pound. Write for brochure giving directions if you're planning a trip to this historic area.

Levine Brothers, Front and Race St., Catasauqua, PA 18032. (About five miles from Allentown.) Phone: (215) 435-3577. Sells wool in five or six pound bags at 40 cents a pound. Variety of weights and colors. Call beforehand.

South Dakota
Northwest Fabrics, 322 S. Vivian St., Aberdeen, SD 57401. Phone: (605) 226-1515. Wool remnants available during most of the fall and winter months.

Virginia
Joan Sealey, 6820 Barnack Drive, Springfield, VA 22152. Phone: (703) 451-6528. Remnants, $2.50 a pound.

Wisconsin
Northwest Fabrics, 2520 Mall Drive, Eau Claire, WI 54701. Phone: (715) 834-9551. Wool remnants available during most of the fall and winter months.

APPENDIX

*Owner at the time photograph was taken.

Homes and homeowners whose dwellings appear in this book:

Craftswomen whose rugs are pictured: